PRACTICE – ASSESS – DIAGNOS

180 Days of
Spelling & Word Study
for Sixth Grade

CH

Author
Shireen Pesez Rhoades, M.A.Ed.

SHELL EDUCATION

Publishing Credits

Corinne Burton, M.A.Ed., *Publisher*
Conni Medina, M.A.Ed., *Editor in Chief*
Emily R. Smith, M.A.Ed., *Content Director*
Véronique Bos, *Creative Director*
Shaun N. Bernadou, *Art Director*
Bianca Marchese, M.S.Ed, *Editor*
Jess Johnson, *Series Graphic Designer*
Evan Ferrell, *Graphic Designer*
Dani Neiley, *Assistant Editor*

Image Credits

All images are from iStock and/or Shutterstock.

Standards

© 2014 Mid-continent Research for Education and Learning
© Copyright 2010. National Governors Association Center for Best Practices and Council of Chief State School Officers. All rights reserved.
© Copyright 2007–2018 Texas Education Agency (TEA). All rights reserved.
© 2007 Teachers of English to Speakers of Other Languages, Inc. (TESOL)
© 2014 Board of Regents of the University of Wisconsin System, on behalf of WIDA— www.wida.us.

Shell Education

A division of Teacher Created Materials
5301 Oceanus Drive
Huntington Beach, CA 92649-1030
www.tcmpub.com/shell-education

ISBN 978-1-4258-3314-5
©2019 Shell Educational Publishing, Inc.

Table of Contents

Introduction

180 Days of Spelling and Word Study provides the missing piece to today's language arts curriculum. Developed by a reading consultant with more than 20 years of classroom and literacy experience, this research-based program is easy to implement, simple to differentiate, and adaptable to any instructional model. The activities are straightforward and engaging. Most importantly, they address today's college and career readiness standards.

This book boosts students' spelling, vocabulary, and decoding skills by familiarizing them with common patterns in a logical, sequential format. Each five-day unit explores a new concept or letter pattern.

Goals of the Series

The first goal of the series is to build students' familiarity with common spelling patterns and rules. The scope and sequence has been designed using a developmental approach, taking into account students' predictive stages of spelling development. Units progress from basic letter sounds to challenging patterns and spiral from one year to the next.

A second goal is to strengthen decoding skills. When students spend a week or more immersed in a particular phonetic pattern, they start to notice and apply the pattern to their daily reading. This program's emphasis on common spelling patterns strengthens students' word-attack skills and helps them break large words into syllables and meaningful chunks.

Introduction (cont.)

Goals of the Series (cont.)

Vocabulary development is the third, and perhaps most critical, goal of the series. Tasks are meaning-based, so students cannot complete them successfully without some knowledge of the words' definitions or parts of speech. Additionally, activities are designed to deepen students' knowledge of targeted words by requiring them to manipulate synonyms, antonyms, and multiple meanings.

Structured Practice

To be successful in spelling, students must focus on the words, word parts, patterns, and definitions. For that reason, this series uses structured practice. Rather than changing the activities week-to-week, the daily activities are repeated throughout the 36 units. That way, students can focus on the words instead of learning how to complete the activities.

The following activities are used throughout this book:

Title of Activity	Description
Analogies	Students use a word bank to complete analogies.
Cursive	Students write spelling words in their best cursive.
Here's the Scenario	Students use a word bank to construct questions or a paragraph based on a given scenario.
Idioms and Proverbs	Students use given words to analyze meanings of idioms and proverbs.
Parts of Speech	Students add or remove suffixes for given words.
Prefixes, Suffixes, and Roots	Students find a Greek or Latin root in the Word Bank words. Then, they match the word to their definitions.
Sentence Completions	Students use a word bank to complete sentences.
Synonyms and Antonyms	Students use a word bank to list synonyms or antonyms of given words.
Turn the Question Around	Students use given words to answer questions in complete sentences. *Turn the Question Around* means restating the question in the answer.
Word Sorts	Students sort words into categories.

How to Use This Book

180 Days of Spelling and Word Study is comprised of 36 units. Each unit revolves around a particular phonetic pattern and includes five separate activities. They can be assigned as homework or morning work, or they can be used as part of a word work rotation. Activities vary throughout each unit.

In this book, students will explore: stressed and unstressed syllables, *r*-controlled vowels, hard and soft consonants, and derivational endings. They will explore common prefixes and suffixes as well as Greek and Latin roots. They will learn how these parts can affect a word's meaning, pronunciation, and part of speech.

Unit Assessments

A list of words is provided at the beginning of each unit. The words share a phonetic pattern that is reinforced in activities throughout the unit. You may choose to send the words home as part of a traditional study list. Additional spelling activities are provided in the Digital Resources. These activities can be specifically assigned, or the whole list can be sent home as a school-home connection.

However, in place of a typical spelling test, you are encouraged to administer the unit quizzes provided on pages 237–238. Each unit quiz contains two words and a dictation sentence. The individual words fit the unit pattern but have not been previously studied. Spelling the words correctly demonstrates that students have mastered the unit's spelling objectives and can apply them to daily work. Further, two to four words in the sentence dictation come from the study list. The rest of the sentence consists of high-frequency or review words. Dictation sentences measure how well students can spell target words in context, while attending to capitalization and punctuation rules.

The units are grouped into categories so you can diagnose how well students understand key phonetic patterns. By grouping these units together in this way, you can record the scores for each unit's assessment within a category and better assess student progress. See the Spelling Categories chart on page 239. You may also choose to record unit assessment scores in the Analysis Charts provided in the Digital Resources. See page 240 for more information.

How to Use This Book *(cont.)*

Differentiating Instruction

Once a phonetic category's assessment results are gathered and analyzed, use the results to inform the way you differentiate instruction. The data can help determine which phonetic patterns are the most difficult for students and which students need additional instructional support and continued practice.

Whole-Class Support

The results of the diagnostic analysis may show that the entire class is struggling with certain phonetic patterns. If they have been taught in the past, this indicates that further instruction or reteaching is necessary. If these patterns have not been taught in the past, this data is a great preassessment and may demonstrate that students do not have a working knowledge of the weekly pattern. Thus, careful planning for reintroducing the words or phonetic patterns may be required.

Small-Group or Individual Support

The results of the diagnostic analysis may also show that an individual student or a small group of students is struggling with certain spelling patterns. If these patterns have been taught in the past, this indicates that further instruction or reteaching is necessary. Consider pulling these students aside to instruct them further while others are working independently. Students may also benefit from extra practice using spelling games or computer-based resources.

You can also use the results to help identify proficient individual students or groups of students who are ready for enrichment or above-level spelling instruction. These students may benefit from independent learning contracts or more challenging words. Additional Spelling Activities are available in the Digital Resources. The activities challenge students to deepen their understanding of spelling patterns.

Included in the Digital Resources are lists of words used in *180 Days of Spelling and Word Study* for grades 5 and 6. These lists can be used for differentiation.

Additional Spelling Activities

The activities included in the Digital Resources offer additional ways to practice the spelling words in each unit. They also make a great school-home connection! See page 240 for more information.

How to Use This Book (cont.)

Word Lists

This chart lists the words and phonetic patterns covered in each unit.

Unit	Words	Spelling Pattern
1	abdomen, acrobat, agony, altitude, astronaut, attitude, Canada, canopy, collaborate, congratulate, contaminate, disaster, evaporate, exaggerate, gratitude, latitude, procrastinate, sacrifice, spatula, stamina	short *a* words
2	dedicate, deficit, demonstrate, elevate, excavate, gentleman, hesitate, investigate, melody, Mexico, parentheses, pedestrian, penalty, precipice, revenue, specimen, stethoscope, surrender, telescope, Texas	short *e* words
3	anticipate, cinnamon, committee, criticize, curriculum, diminish, disintegrate, eclipse, eliminate, exquisite, illustrate, imitate, immigrate, indicate, industry, intellect, isthmus, participate, peninsula, stringent	short *i* words
4	acronym, chrysalis, cymbals, cynical, encrypted, gymnastics, larynx, mystify, pseudonym, pyramid, symbolic, symmetry, sympathy, syndrome, synopsis, syntax, synthesize, synthetic, syrup, typical	more short *i* words
5	accommodate, compensate, complicated, comprehend, consolidate, cooperate, dominate, economy, hippopotamus, misconduct, modify, molecule, nominate, obstacle, omnivore, poverty, prosecute, rhombus, thermometer, volatile	short *o* words
6	apparel, aquarium, area, caramel, caravan, charity, clarify, comparison, disparage, disparity, marathon, marinate, mascara, parachute, paradise, parallel, paralyze, popularity, scenario, similarity	*ar* pattern
7	America, controversy, currency, Europe, formula, herbivore, interfere, introverted, irritate, journalist, merchandise, organize, purposely, quarantine, refurbish, sincerely, terminate, thermostat, versatile, warranty	*r*-controlled vowels
8	advertisement, amendment, announcement, arrangement, attachment, commitment, development, disagreement, disappointment, encouragement, environment, establishment, excitement, implement, involvement, management, measurement, sediment, settlement, supplement	*–ment* ending
9	adhesive, aggressive, alternative, assertive, competitive, comprehensive, consecutive, cooperative, decorative, destructive, excessive, executive, extensive, figurative, imaginative, informative, interactive, possessive, primitive, representative	*–ive* ending
10	alligator, ambassador, calculator, career, caterpillar, competitor, denominator, educator, elevator, engineer, escalator, illustrator, investor, muscular, numerator, particular, pioneer, professor, realtor, refrigerator	*–ar*, *–er*, and *–or* endings
11	admiration, cancellation, combination, conservation, conversation, declaration, expiration, exploration, imagination, information, inspiration, invitation, observation, organization, perspiration, presentation, preservation, reservation, transformation, transportation	*–ation* ending

Unit	Words	Spelling Pattern
12	abbreviation, application, communication, congratulations, constitution, decoration, evaporation, inauguration, institution, investigation, legislation, multiplication, notification, participation, qualifications, recreation, resolution, revolution, solution, unification	more –*tion* endings
13	aggression, apprehension, commission, comprehension, concessions, concussion, depression, diversion, excursion, illusion, incision, obsession, persuasion, precision, procession, progression, provisions, supervision, suspension, television	–*sion* ending
14	charitable, comfortable, comparable, considerable, inevitable, irritable, knowledgeable, manageable, memorable, noticeable, perishable, probable, reasonable, remarkable, respectable, unavoidable, unbelievable, undependable, variables, vulnerable	–*able* ending
15	compatible, convertible, distractible, divisible, eligible, feasible, illegible, impossible, incredible, indelible, indestructible, indivisible, infallible, inflexible, invincible, invisible, irresistible, irreversible, responsible, reversible	–*ible* ending
16	academic, aerobic, Antarctic, antibiotic, Arctic, authentic, automatic, ceramic, democratic, domestic, dramatic, economics, energetic, epidemic, exotic, majestic, pathetic, patriotic, sympathetic, traumatic	–*ic* ending
17	alphabetical, carnival, collateral, critical, emotional, horizontal, hysterical, intentional, international, interval, literal, maternal, nocturnal, numeral, paternal, perpetual, practical, rehearsal, terminal, universal	–*al* ending
18	abundant, appliance, arrogance, attendance, buoyancy, defiant, discrepancy, endurance, extravagant, ignorant, insurance, maintenance, observant, occupancy, pregnancy, redundant, reluctant, resistant, significant, vacancy	–*ant* and –*ance* endings
19	affluent, apparent, competent, condolences, consequence, consistency, eloquent, equivalent, frequency, incompetent, independence, indifferent, interference, permanent, persistent, preference, presidency, prevalent, superintendent, turbulence	–*ent* and –*ence* endings
20	adequate, advocate, affectionate, approximate, articulate, associate, compassionate, coordinate, desolate, duplicate, illiterate, immaculate, inanimate, inappropriate, intermediate, intricate, legitimate, moderate, unfortunate, vertebrate	–*ate* ending
21	authority, capacity, curiosity, electricity, equality, facility, fidelity, hospitality, hostility, humidity, intensity, nationality, necessity, opportunity, personality, possibility, priority, responsibility, security, university	–*ity* ending
22	anniversary, capillary, commentary, complimentary, culinary, customary, documentary, exemplary, extraordinary, hereditary, imaginary, infirmary, involuntary, itinerary, monetary, obituary, revolutionary, salivary, sanitary, vocabulary	–*ary* ending
23	accessory, accusatory, auditory, circulatory, contradictory, derogatory, discriminatory, dormitory, inflammatory, introductory, laboratory, lavatory, migratory, obligatory, observatory, predatory, respiratory, satisfactory, self-explanatory, trajectory	–*ory* ending

Unit	Words	Spelling Pattern
24	adventurous, autonomous, carnivorous, disastrous, frivolous, herbivorous, indigenous, ludicrous, meticulous, miraculous, mischievous, mountainous, ominous, omnivorous, perilous, prosperous, ridiculous, synonymous, unanimous, villainous	*–ous* ending
25	analogy, apology, archaeology, biology, chronology, disadvantage, ecology, epilogue, geologist, geology, intriguing, meteorology, monologue, mythology, psychologist, psychology, synagogue, technology, terminology, zoology	hard and soft *g* words
26	anterior, bacteria, cafeteria, clerical, criteria, deteriorate, experience, experiment, exterior, imperial, inferior, interior, material, mysterious, period, posterior, serial, severity, superior, ulterior	*eri* pattern
27	alleviate, audience, colonial, custodian, disobedient, equilibrium, gymnasium, humiliate, idiom, idiosyncrasy, marsupial, memorial, menial, nutrients, podium, portfolio, radiant, radius, recipient, trivial	more *i* patterns that sound like *e*
28	appreciation, association, atrocious, beneficial, depreciate, electrician, insufficient, judicious, magician, malicious, mathematician, musician, pediatrician, physician, politician, sociable, specialty, suspicious, technician, unconscious	*ci* words
29	ambitious, anxious, cautious, conscientious, contagious, courageous, gorgeous, hilarious, igneous, industrious, miscellaneous, nutritious, outrageous, prestigious, rambunctious, religious, scrumptious, spontaneous, superstitious, victorious	*–eous* and *–ious* endings
30	Asian, Christian, confidential, controversial, credential, essential, influential, initial, initiative, negotiate, partial, patience, patient, potential, preferential, quotient, residential, sequential, substantial, torrential	more *ti* and *si* patterns
31	acquaintance, antique, banquet, bouquet, boutique, clique, conquer, critique, croquet, delinquent, etiquette, grotesque, mosque, oblique, opaque, picturesque, plaque, technique, tourniquet, unique	*qu* pattern
32	agility, allegiance, allergen, congenital, detergent, digital, diligent, generic, generosity, geometry, indulgent, legendary, legislature, manageable, negligent, nostalgic, prodigious, pungent, regional, strategy	more soft *g* words
33	amphibian, apostrophe, biography, catastrophe, decipher, esophagus, geography, metamorphosis, peripheral, pharmacist, phenomenon, philosophy, photocopy, photographer, photosynthesis, physical, sophisticated, sophomore, triumphant, xylophone	*ph* words
34	accentuate, accessible, accidentally, adolescent, celebration, celebrity, circumstances, coincidence, condescending, convalescent, descendant, eccentric, fascination, fluorescent, necessary, publicity, reminisce, scientific, succinctly, susceptible	more soft *c* patterns
35	arachnid, architect, archives, bronchitis, chameleon, chaos, character, characteristics, charisma, chemical, chemistry, choreograph, chronic, chronological, chrysalis, mechanic, monarch, orchestra, scholarship, technical	hard *ch* words
36	brochure, chagrin, chalet, chandelier, chaperone, charade, chauffeur, chef, Chicago, chiffon, chivalrous, cliché, crochet, fuchsia, machinery, Michigan, mustache, nonchalant, pistachio, quiche	soft *ch* words

Standards Correlations

Shell Education is committed to producing educational materials that are research and standards based. All products are correlated to the academic standards of all 50 states, the District of Columbia, the Department of Defense Dependent Schools, and the Canadian provinces.

How to Find Standards Correlations

To print a customized correlation report of this product for your state, visit **www.tcmpub.com/administrators/correlations/** and follow the online directions. If you require assistance in printing correlation reports, please contact the Customer Service Department at 1-877-777-3450.

Purpose and Intent of Standards

The Every Student Succeeds Act (ESSA) mandates that all states adopt challenging academic standards that help students meet the goal of college and career readiness. While many states already adopted academic standards prior to ESSA, the act continues to hold states accountable for detailed and comprehensive standards.

Standards are designed to focus instruction and guide adoption of curricula. Standards are statements that describe the criteria necessary for students to meet specific academic goals. They define the knowledge, skills, and content students should acquire at each level. Standards are also used to develop standardized tests to evaluate students' academic progress. Teachers are required to demonstrate how their lessons meet state standards. State standards are used in the development of all Shell products, so educators can be assured they meet the academic requirements of each state.

College and Career Readiness

In this book, the following college and career readiness (CCR) standard is met: Spell grade-appropriate words correctly, consulting references as needed.

McREL Compendium

Each year, McREL analyzes state standards and revises the compendium to produce a general compilation of national standards. In this book, the following standards are met: Demonstrate command of the conventions of standard English capitalization, punctuation, and spelling when writing; spell grade-appropriate words correctly, consulting references as needed.

TESOL and WIDA Standards

In this book, the following English language development standards are met: Standard 1: English language learners communicate for social and instructional purposes within the school setting. Standard 2: English language learners communicate information, ideas, and concepts necessary for academic success in the content area of language arts.

UNIT 4
More Short *I* Words

- acronym
- chrysalis
- cymbals
- cynical
- encrypted
- gymnastics
- larynx
- mystify
- pseudonym
- pyramid
- symbolic
- symmetry
- sympathy
- syndrome
- synopsis
- syntax
- synthesize
- synthetic
- syrup
- typical

Focus

This week's focus is on multisyllabic words that use *y* to make the short *i* sound.

Helpful Hint

Notice that all the words on this list contain a short *i* sound that is represented by the letter *y*. The letter *y* only makes a short *i* sound when it is surrounded by consonants (*sym·bol·ic, typ·i·cal*). Notice that the *y* sound changes slightly when it is followed by the letter *r* (*syr·up, pyr·a·mid*).

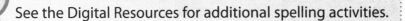

See the Digital Resources for additional spelling activities.

Name: _____ **Date:** _____

Sentence Completions

Directions: Use a word from the Word Bank to complete each sentence.

Word Bank			
acronym	chrysalis	cymbals	encrypted
pseudonym	symbolic	symmetry	sympathy
syndrome	synopsis	synthesize	synthetic

1. Many of my parents' friends sent _____ cards and flowers when my grandfather died.

2. Zahra plays the _____ in our school marching band.

3. Did you know that some authors use a _____ , or fake name, when they write books?

4. My cousin was born with a rare _____ that affected his lungs and digestive system.

5. How many lines of _____ are in an equilateral triangle?

6. Angela is allergic to _____ fabrics, such as spandex and nylon.

7. NASA is an _____ that stands for National Aeronautics and Space Administration.

8. We are waiting for one more butterfly to emerge from its _____ .

9. *The Giving Tree* is a _____ book because the tree represents a parent's unending love.

10. Military messages are _____ so no one can intercept and read them.

11. Just give me a brief _____ of the movie. Don't tell me every detail.

12. You need to collect all the data and then _____ it to write your report.

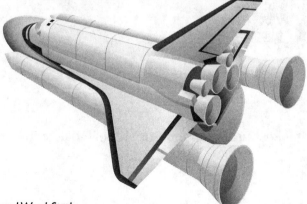

Name: _____ **Date:** _____

Directions: Use a word from the Word Bank for each section.

Word Bank			
acronym	cymbals	cynical	encrypted
larynx	mystify	pyramid	syndrome
synthesize	synthetic	syrup	typical

Write a synonym for each word or phrase.

1. voice box _____

2. abbreviation _____

3. coded _____

4. combine _____

Write an antonym for each word.

5. trusting _____

6. unusual _____

7. clarify _____

8. natural _____

Write a word that fits each category.

9. drums, xylophone, tambourine, _____

10. sauce, dressing, gravy, _____

11. cube, cylinder, rectangular prism, _____

12. disease, condition, disorder, _____

Prefixes, Suffixes, and Roots

Name: _____ Date: _____

Directions: The root *syn* is a prefix that means *with* or *together*. The prefix is assimilated because it changes depending on the first letter of the word it joins. It can become *syl–*, *sym–*, or *sys–*. Use a word from the Word Bank to match each definition.

Word Bank			
syllables	symbol	symmetry	sympathy
symphony	symptoms	sync	syndrome
synopsis	syntax	synthesize	synthetic

1. _____ **shared** feelings of kindness and compassion, especially during times of sadness (*noun*)

2. _____ word chunks with one vowel sound that go **together** to form a word (*noun*)

3. _____ link two devices **together** so they can share information—shortened form (*verb*)

4. _____ the quality of having matching parts when the sides of an object are folded **together** (*noun*)

5. _____ the music that is created when instruments play **together** in an orchestra (*noun*)

6. _____ an object that represents, stands for, or goes **with** something else (*noun*)

7. _____ physical clues that go **together** to prove a person is sick (*noun*)

8. _____ a brief outline or summary that **includes** only the most important details (*noun*)

9. _____ the way words fit **together** to form a logical sentence (*noun*)

10. _____ combine; put ideas, sounds, or substances **together** to make something new (*verb*)

11. _____ made from ingredients that have been put **together** to create a new, artificial substance (*adjective*)

12. _____ a medical condition that has several signs or symptoms that go **together** (*noun*)

Name: _____ **Date:** _____

Directions: Write 10 of the words from the Word Bank two times each in your best cursive.

Word Bank				
acronym	chrysalis	cymbals	cynical	encrypted
gymnastics	larynx	mystify	pseudonym	pyramid
symbolic	symmetry	sympathy	syndrome	synopsis
syntax	synthesize	synthetic	syrup	typical

Name: _____   **Date:** _____

Analogies

Directions: Use a word from the Word Bank to complete each analogy.

Word Bank			
acronym	chrysalis	cymbals	gymnastics
larynx	pseudonym	pyramids	symbolic
sympathy	syntax	synthetic	syrup

1.   **sundae** is to **chocolate sauce** as **waffles** is to _____

2.   **China** is to **Great Wall** as **Egypt** is to _____

3.   **moth** is to **cocoon** as **butterfly** is to _____

4.   **cotton** is to **natural** as **polyester** is to _____

5.   **type of words** is to **grammar** as **arrangement of words** is to _____

6.   **laugh out loud** is to **phrase** as **LOL** is to _____

7.   **Theodor Geisel** is to **real name** as **Dr. Seuss** is to _____

8.   **Winter Olympics** is to **ice skating** as **Summer Olympics** is to _____

9.   **windpipe** is to **trachea** as **voice box** is to _____

10. **wedding** is to **congratulations** as **funeral** is to _____

11. **clap** is to **hands** as **play** is to _____

12. **key ring** is to **functional** as **wedding ring** is to _____

UNIT 5
Short O Words

Focus

This week's focus is on multisyllabic words with a stressed short *o* syllable.

Helpful Hint

Notice that the stressed syllable in each word has a short *o* sound (*com·pen·sate, e·con·o·my*). Some of the words on this week's list begin with a variant of the *com–* prefix, which means *with* or *at the same time*.

- accommodate
- compensate
- complicated
- comprehend
- consolidate
- cooperate
- dominate
- economy
- hippopotamus
- misconduct
- modify
- molecule
- nominate
- obstacle
- omnivore
- poverty
- prosecute
- rhombus
- thermometer
- volatile

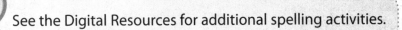

See the Digital Resources for additional spelling activities.

Sentence Completions

Name: _____ Date: _____

Directions: Use a word from the Word Bank to complete each sentence.

Word Bank			
accommodate	compensate	consolidate	dominate
economy	modify	molecule	nominate
obstacle	poverty	prosecute	volatile

1. We called the restaurant to see if they could _____ a party of ten.

2. They need to switch up the teams so the Oilers don't _____ every season.

3. The store will _____ if they catch you shoplifting.

4. We decided to _____ our resources to build a better clubhouse.

5. My project is almost done. I just need to _____ a couple of the photos and captions.

6. I'm going to _____ Keiko for class president because I know she'd do a great job.

7. We set up an _____ course in the backyard with planks, hula hoops, and old tires.

8. The situation is _____ . Another battle could erupt at any moment.

9. More people buy homes and invest in new businesses when the region's

   _____ is strong.

10. Will your boss _____ you for all the extra hours you spent on this project?

11. A _____ is so small, you need a powerful microscope to see it.

12. One way to fight _____ is by making sure all children get a great education.

Name: _____ **Date:** _____

Directions: Use a word from the Word Bank for each section.

Word Bank

compensate	complicated	consolidate	cooperate
misconduct	modify	omnivore	poverty
prosecute	rhombus	thermometer	volatile

Write a synonym for each word or phrase.

1. change
   slightly _____

2. combine _____

3. work
   together _____

4. explosive _____

Write an antonym for each word or phrase.

5. good
   behavior _____

6. wealth _____

7. simple _____

8. drop the
   charges _____

Write a word that fits each category.

9. scale, ruler, measuring cup, _____

10. parallelogram, trapezoid, triangle, _____

11. pay, reimburse, reward, _____

12. herbivore, carnivore, insectivore, _____

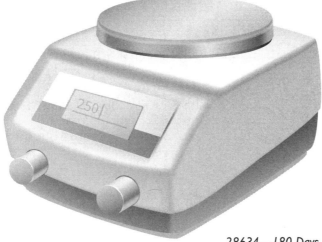

Synonyms and Antonyms

Name: _____ Date:_____

Directions: Add a form of the *com–* prefix to each word or root to create a real word.

1. operate   _____
2. ordinate   _____
3. exist   _____
4. incidence   _____
5. ed   _____

6. pensate   _____
7. plicate   _____
8. prehend   _____
9. solidate   _____
10. duct   _____

> The prefix *com–* means *with* or *at the same time*. The *com–* prefix is assimilated because it changes depending on the first letter of the word it joins. It can become *con–*, *cor–*, *col–*, or *co–* depending on the letter that follows. Add *com–* to words or roots that start with *b*, *m*, or *p*. Add *co–* to words that start with a vowel or the letter *h*. Add *col–* to words that start with *l*, and *cor–* to words that start with *r*. For most other letters, the prefix changes to *con–*.

Directions: Choose a word from the answers above to complete each sentence.

11. My school is _____ , but my neighbor goes to a school that is just for boys.

12. What a _____ ! I can't believe all three of us are getting our braces on the same day!

13. My parents always remind me to _____ myself appropriately at a restaurant.

14. Dad offered to _____ our neighbors for their mailbox after he backed into it.

15. If my school play and my sister's prom are on the same night, that could _____ things.

16. If you _____ with the nurse when she gives you a shot, it'll be quick and painless.

17. I can't _____ this show. It's like a foreign language to me.

18. Our cat and dog _____ in the house but don't really pay attention to each other.

Name: _____ **Date:** _____

Directions: Answer each question in a complete sentence. Remember to turn the question around, and use the bold word in your answer.

1. Why should you **compensate** your friend if you break something that belongs to him or her?

    _____

    _____

2. How do schools **accommodate** students in wheelchairs?

    _____

    _____

3. What **obstacles** might you face if you tried to sail across the ocean?

    _____

    _____

4. Should parents be **prosecuted** if their child commits a crime? Explain.

    _____

    _____

5. Why do **thermometers** have two sets of numbers on them?

    _____

    _____

6. What are three examples of **omnivores**?

    _____

    _____

Turn the Question Around

Name: _____ **Date:** _____

Directions: Use a word from the Word Bank to complete each analogy.

Word Bank			
complicated	consolidate	economy	hippopotamus
misconduct	nominate	omnivore	poverty
prosecute	rhombus	thermometer	volatile

1. **weight** is to **scale** as **temperature** is to _____

2. **meat** is to **carnivore** as **meat and plants** is to _____

3. **weaken** is to **spread out** as **strengthen** is to _____

4. **lack of food** is to **famine** as **lack of money** is to _____

5. **five sides** is to **pentagon** as **four sides** is to _____

6. **president** is to **elect** as **candidate** is to _____

7. **doctors** is to **health** as **bankers** is to _____

8. **horns** is to **rhinoceros** as **no horns** is to _____

9. **2 + 2** is to **basic** as **3(5a + 2a²)** is to _____

10. **reward** is to **good behavior** as **punish** is to _____

11. **peaceful country** is to **stable** as **war zone** is to _____

12. **misconduct** is to **punish** as **crime** is to _____

UNIT 6
ar Pattern

Focus

This week's focus is on multisyllabic words that use *ar* to make an /air/ sound.

Helpful Hint

Notice that all the words on this list contain an *ar* syllable that is pronounced /air/. In these words, the *ar* pattern is always preceded by a consonant or digraph (*char·i·ty*, *par·al·lel*, *sce·nar·i·o*). Notice how the pronunciation of the base word changes when a suffix is added (*popular/popularity*, *similar/similarity*).

- apparel
- aquarium
- area
- caramel
- caravan
- charity
- clarify
- comparison
- disparage
- disparity
- marathon
- marinate
- mascara
- parachute
- paradise
- parallel
- paralyze
- popularity
- scenario
- similarity

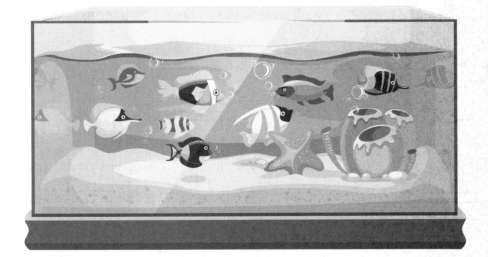

 See the Digital Resources for additional spelling activities.

Name: _____ Date: _____

Directions: Use a word from the Word Bank to complete each sentence.

Sentence Completions

Word Bank			
apparel	caravan	charity	clarify
comparison	disparage	disparity	marinate
parallel	paralyze	popularity	scenario

1. Every rectangle has two pairs of _____ sides.

2. Why is there such a huge _____ between the amount of money athletes and soldiers get paid?

3. Try not to worry so much about _____ . Just be yourself and people will like you.

4. A _____ of covered wagons left Missouri in May 1844 and arrived in Oregon in September.

5. Reporters asked the senator to _____ statements he made earlier about immigration.

6. Jokes that _____ an ethnic, racial, or religious group will not be permitted at the talent show.

7. Worst-case _____ , we'll have to move the wedding reception indoors.

8. All the store's summer _____ has been marked down to make room for fall fashions.

9. The March of Dimes is my favorite _____ because they raise money to help babies.

10. The medicine will _____ the nerve in the tooth for a few hours.

11. There is no _____ between thin crust and deep dish pizza because deep dish clearly tastes better!

12. Mom asked me to get the steak so she could _____ it in a secret blend of sauces and spices before grilling it.

Name: _____ **Date:** _____

Directions: Use a word from the Word Bank for each section.

Word Bank			
apparel	area	caramel	charity
clarify	disparage	marinate	mascara
paradise	parallel	popularity	scenario

Write a synonym for each word or phrase.

1. situation _____

2. clothing _____

3. soak _____

4. bliss _____

5. nonprofit
   organization _____

Write an antonym for each word or phrase.

6. perpendicular _____

7. confuse _____

8. compliment _____

9. lack of
   friends _____

Write a word that fits each category.

10. eyeliner, lip gloss, powder, _____

11. perimeter, volume, length, _____

12. butterscotch, chocolate, marshmallow, _____

Name: _____ **Date:** _____

Prefixes, Suffixes, and Roots

Directions: The root *par* comes from a Latin word that means *equal*. The prefix *para–* means *beside* or *near*. Use a word from the Word Bank to match each definition.

Word Bank			
comparable	compare	disparage	disparaging
disparity	incomparable	paragraph	paralegal
parallel	paramedic	paraphrase	parasite

1. _____ a person who assists and works **beside** a lawyer (*noun*)

2. _____ a person who assists and works **beside** a doctor, especially on the way to the hospital (*noun*)

3. _____ describing two lines or objects that are **side by side** but never cross (*adjective*)

4. _____ an organism that lives in or **near** another animal to steal its nutrients (*noun*)

5. _____ restate a story or conversation in a way that is **near** the original (*verb*)

6. _____ a group of sentences that are placed **near** each other because they relate to the same topic (*noun*)

7. _____ insult or degrade; make a person feel less than **equal** (*verb*)

8. _____ insulting; referring to remarks that make a person feel less than **equal** (*adjective*)

9. _____ determine if two items are similar or of **equal** value (*verb*)

10. _____ similar; of **equal** value (*adjective*)

11. _____ better than anything else; having no **equal** (*adjective*)

12. _____ a lack of **equality** or consistency (*noun*)

Name: _____   Date:_____

Directions: Answer each question in a complete sentence. Remember to turn the question around, and use the bold word in your answer.

1. Which stores sell your favorite **apparel**?

    _____

    _____

2. Why do people **marinate** meat before grilling it?

    _____

    _____

3. What is your favorite **charity**? Why?

    _____

    _____

4. What are some **similarities** between bubbles and balloons?

    _____

    _____

5. What babysitting **scenario** might require you to call 911?

    _____

    _____

6. How do you find the **area** of a rectangle?

    _____

    _____

Analogies

Name: _____   Date:_____

Directions: Use a word from the Word Bank to complete each analogy.

Word Bank			
apparel	aquarium	area	caramel
charity	clarify	disparage	marathon
marinate	mascara	parachute	parallel

1. **cross at 90°** is to **perpendicular** as **never cross** is to _____

2. **lips** is to **lipstick** as **eyelashes** is to _____

3. **short distance** is to **sprint** as **long distance** is to _____

4. **monkeys** is to **zoo** as **manta rays** is to _____

5. **make confusing** is to **muddle** as **make clear** is to _____

6. **say nice things** is to **compliment** as **say mean things** is to _____

7. **grocery store** is to **food** as **department store** is to _____

8. **captain** is to **lifeboat** as **pilot** is to _____

9. **raw beans** is to **soak** as **raw meat** is to _____

10. **pay** is to **tax collector** as **donate** is to _____

11. **amount of fencing** is to **perimeter** as **amount of topsoil** is to _____

12. **burger** is to **mustard** as **sundae** is to _____

UNIT 7
R-Controlled Vowels

- America
- controversy
- currency
- Europe
- formula
- herbivore
- interfere
- introverted
- irritate
- journalist
- merchandise
- organize
- purposely
- quarantine
- refurbish
- sincerely
- terminate
- thermostat
- versatile
- warranty

Focus

This week's focus is on multisyllabic words that use an *r*-controlled vowel to make the /ar/, /er/, or /or/ sound.

Helpful Hint

Notice that all the words on this list contain an *r*-controlled vowel. Some of the *ar*, *er*, *or*, and *ur* patterns are regular and predictable (*mer·chan·dise, or·gan·ize, cur·ren·cy*). Some of the patterns are less common and irregular (*quar·ran·tine, war·ran·ty, sin·cere·ly, ir·ri·tate*).

See the Digital Resources for additional spelling activities.

Name: _____ Date: _____

Directions: Use a word from the Word Bank to complete each sentence.

Word Bank			
controversy	currency	formula	irritate
merchandise	purposely	quarantine	refurbish
terminate	thermostat	versatile	warranty

Sentence Completions

1. The 20% off coupon only works on full-price _____ , not sale items.

2. The phone company will _____ your service if you don't pay your monthly bill.

3. Dad sets the _____ lower at night since we're all wrapped under blankets.

4. There was some _____ about the umpire's call at first base.

5. My uncle brings me _____ from every country he visits so I can add it to my money collection.

6. I had to memorize the _____ for finding the area of a circle. Now I know it!

7. I like to buy old wooden crates and _____ them to look brand new.

8. This jack knife is such a _____ tool. You can use it to cut, open, twist, or clip things.

9. Adam _____ pushed me into a puddle. Now my socks and sneakers are soaking wet!

10. It is best to _____ a new fish for a few days so it doesn't get the other fish in the tank sick.

11. I don't like wearing wool sweaters because they _____ my skin.

12. I paid extra for the _____ , so if anything happens to my phone, they'll give me a new one.

Name: _____ Date: _____

Directions: Use a word from the Word Bank for each section.

Word Bank			
America	Europe	formula	interfere
introverted	irritate	organize	purposely
refurbish	sincerely	terminate	versatile

Write a synonym for each word or phrase.

1. adaptable _____

2. meddle _____

3. United States _____

4. arrange _____

Write an antonym for each word.

5. accidentally _____

6. extroverted _____

7. start _____

8. soothe _____

Write a word that fits each category.

9. recipe, method, series of steps, _____

10. Asia, Africa, South America, _____

11. love, yours truly, your friend, _____

12. fix up, renovate, restore, _____

© Shell Education

28634—180 Days of Spelling and Word Study

49

Prefixes, Suffixes, and Roots

Name: _____   Date: _____

Directions: *Vers* and *vert* are Latin roots that mean *turn*. Use a word from the Word Bank to match each definition.

Word Bank			
anniversary	aversion	controversial	conversation
convert	diversion	introverted	invert
reverse	universe	versatile	version

1. _____ a discussion; a time when people take **turns** talking (*noun*)

2. _____ move backwards; **turn** back (*verb*)

3. _____ a distraction; something that **turns** your attention to something else (*noun*)

4. _____ the whole world, **turned** into one (*noun*)

5. _____ the date on which a relationship or event **turns** a year older (*noun*)

6. _____ a story or game that has been **turned** into something slightly different (*noun*)

7. _____ **turn** or flip upside down, such as a fraction or a cake pan (*verb*)

8. _____ **turn** or change your beliefs or religion (*verb*)

9. _____ a strong dislike; an overwhelming urge to **turn** away from something (*noun*)

10. _____ likely to spark opposing views and **turn** people against each other (*adjective*)

11. _____ **turned** inward; not sociable or outgoing (*adjective*)

12. _____ having many uses or purposes; **turning** with ease from one thing to another (*adjective*)

Name: _____   Date:_____

Directions: Answer each question in a complete sentence. Remember to turn the question around, and use the bold word in your answer.

1. Why is it important for band teachers to be **versatile** musicians?

    _____

    _____

2. Why do people spend extra money on **warranties** for their electronics?

    _____

    _____

3. Why do stores put security tags on their **merchandise**?

    _____

    _____

4. Do you think you're more of an **introvert** or extrovert? Explain.

    _____

    _____

5. When should parents **interfere** with arguing children?

    _____

    _____

6. Why is it important to stay **organized**?

    _____

    _____

Turn the Question Around

Analogies

Name: _____ Date: _____

Directions: Use a word from the Word Bank to complete each analogy.

Word Bank			
America	currency	Europe	herbivore
interfere	introverted	journalist	organized
quarantine	sincerely	thermostat	warranty

1. **Pakistan** is to **Asia** as **Sweden** is to _____

2. **books** is to **author** as **articles** is to _____

3. **dirty room** is to **cleaned** as **messy room** is to _____

4. **speed** is to **speedometer** as **temperature** is to _____

5. **meat** is to **carnivore** as **plants** is to _____

6. **greeting** is to **dear** as **closing** is to _____

7. **outgoing** is to **extroverted** as **shy** is to _____

8. **jurors** is to **sequester** as **sick people** is to _____

9. **maple leaf** is to **Canada** as **stars and stripes** is to _____

10. **product instructions** is to **manual** as **product protection** is to _____

11. **peacemaker** is to **intervene** as **meddler** is to _____

12. **shirt** is to **apparel** as **dollar** is to _____

UNIT 8
–ment Ending

Focus

This week's focus is on multisyllabic words that end with –*ment*. The derivational suffix –*ment* changes a verb to a noun.

Helpful Hint

Notice that all the words on this list end with –*ment*. The –*ment* suffix changes a verb to a noun. For example, *arrange* becomes *arrangement*, and *measure* becomes *measurement*. Do not drop the silent *e* when adding a suffix that starts with a consonant (–*ment*, –*ful*, –*ness*, –*ly*, etc.). Two words on this list (*implement*, *supplement*) can be used either as a verb or a noun.

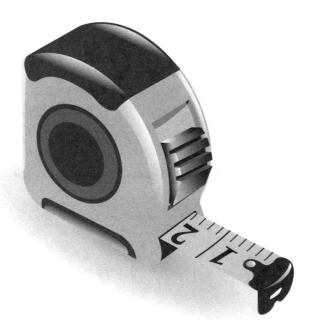

See the Digital Resources for additional spelling activities.

- advertisement
- amendment
- announcement
- arrangement
- attachment
- commitment
- development
- disagreement
- disappointment
- encouragement
- environment
- establishment
- excitement
- implement
- involvement
- management
- measurement
- sediment
- settlement
- supplement

Name: _____ Date: _____

Directions: Use a word from the Word Bank to complete each sentence.

Sentence Completions

Word Bank			
amendment	arrangement	attachment	commitment
development	encouragement	environment	establishment
implement	management	sediment	supplement

1. We made an _____ to our class constitution.

2. The school had to _____ new pick-up and drop-off procedures to keep students safe.

3. We are learning about human growth and _____ in health class.

4. If you don't like the furniture _____, you can move your bed back against the window.

5. Open the coach's email, and you'll see an _____ that lists all the game dates and times.

6. The _____ of a new post office in town will make it easier for people to mail packages.

7. Rita started her career as a file clerk and worked her way up to a _____ position.

8. Akira decided to _____ her income with a second waitressing job.

9. You can't quit soccer now. You've already made a _____ to your coach and teammates.

10. Deltas form when sand, pebbles, and other types of _____ settle at the mouth of a river.

11. Thanks to your kind words of _____, I've decided to run for class president!

12. Read the label carefully. Some lawn chemicals and fertilizers are harmful to the _____.

Name: _____ **Date:** _____

Directions: Use a word from the Word Bank for each section.

Word Bank

advertisement	announcement	attachment	development
disappointment	encouragement	environment	excitement
implement	involvement	settlement	supplement

Write a synonym for each word or phrase.

1. surroundings _____
2. colony _____
3. growth _____
4. connection _____
5. put into action _____
6. participation _____

Write an antonym for each word.

7. discouragement _____
8. dread _____
9. satisfaction _____

Write a word that fits each category.

10. commercial, coupon, special offer, _____

11. declaration, broadcast, proclamation, _____

12. add to, increase, build on, _____

© Shell Education

28634—180 Days of Spelling and Word Study

55

Synonyms and Antonyms

Name: _____ **Date:** _____

Directions: Did you know that *volv and volut* come from a Latin word that means *roll* or *turn around*? Use a word from the Word Bank to match each definition.

Word Bank				
convoluted	devolve	evolution	evolve	involve
involvement	revolution	revolve	revolver	volume

1. _____ **turn** or **roll** around an axis, such as a planet or Ferris wheel (*verb*)

2. _____ a type of weapon that has a **turning** cylinder (*noun*)

3. _____ an overthrow of government that causes everything to **turn around** (*noun*)

4. _____ **roll** into a better or more advanced state (*verb*)

5. _____ the process of **rolling** slowly into a better or more advanced state (*noun*)

6. _____ **roll** into a worse state, such as a bad relationship (*verb*)

7. _____ take part in something; **roll** into a situation (*verb*)

8. _____ the act of **rolling** into a situation (*noun*)

9. _____ the amount of space something takes up; originally, the size of a **rolled**-up piece of parchment (*noun*)

10. _____ complex and confusing, such as a story that has many twists and **turns** (*adjective*)

Prefixes, Suffixes, and Roots

Name: _____ **Date:** _____

Directions: You are a reporter for the local news station. Your boss wants you to interview the police chief, who is celebrating his 25th year on the force. What are some questions you'd like to ask him? Write six questions for the police chief on the lines below. Use at least one *–ment* word in each sentence.

Word Bank				
accomplishment	achievement	agreement	announcement	argument
assignment	commitment	compliment	department	development
disagreement	enforcement	environment	equipment	improvement
management	moment	replacement	retirement	statement

● _____

_____

● _____

_____

_____

● _____

_____

● _____

_____

● _____

_____

● _____

_____

Name: _____ **Date:** _____

Directions: Use a word from the Word Bank to complete each analogy.

Word Bank

advertisement	amendment	announcement	development
disagreement	disappointment	environment	excitement
implement	measurement	sediment	settlement

1. **bottom of cookie jar** is to **crumbs** as **bottom of river** is to _____

2. **TV** is to **commercial** as **magazine** is to _____

3. **improve a book** is to **revision** as **improve a law** is to _____

4. **Veterans Day** is to **Armed Forces** as **Earth Day** is to _____

5. **colonists** is to **colony** as **settlers** is to _____

6. **thermometer** is to **temperature** as **ruler** is to _____

7. **waiting for punishment** is to **dread** as **waiting for a friend** is to _____

8. **new appliances** is to **install** as **new policies** is to _____

9. **nod your head** is to **agreement** as **shake your head** is to _____

10. **alarm system** is to **warning** as **loudspeaker** is to _____

11. **death of a pet** is to **devastation** as **missing a field trip** is to _____

12. **group of people** is to **crowd** as **group of houses** is to _____

UNIT 9
–ive Ending

Focus

This week's focus is on multisyllabic words that end with –*ive*. This derivational suffix changes a verb to an adjective.

Helpful Hint

Notice that all the words on this list end with –*ive*. The –*ive* suffix changes a verb to an adjective. For example, *cooperate* becomes *cooperative*, and *interact* becomes *interactive*. Sometimes an extra syllable is added between the base word and suffix (*represent/representative*, *imagine/imaginative*), and sometimes the base word changes slightly (*extend/extensive*, *comprehend/comprehensive*).

> - adhesive
> - aggressive
> - alternative
> - assertive
> - competitive
> - comprehensive
> - consecutive
> - cooperative
> - decorative
> - destructive
> - excessive
> - executive
> - extensive
> - figurative
> - imaginative
> - informative
> - interactive
> - possessive
> - primitive
> - representative

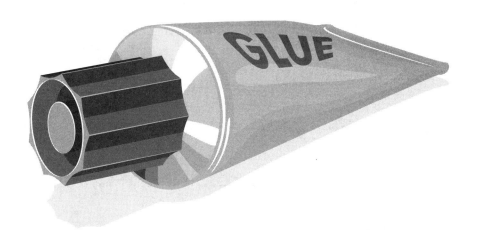

See the Digital Resources for additional spelling activities.

Sentence Completions

Name: _____ Date: _____

Directions: Use a word from the Word Bank to complete each sentence.

Word Bank			
adhesive	alternative	assertive	competitive
consecutive	decorative	excessive	executive
extensive	figurative	primitive	representative

1. Ancient civilizations created _____ tools out of sticks, rocks, and animal bones.

2. I don't enjoy _____ sports. I prefer to hike and swim instead.

3. The _____ branch of government is in charge of enforcing our nation's laws.

4. After an _____ search of the entire playground, we still couldn't find Josiah's house key.

5. My sister's too young to stay home alone, so our only _____ is to bring her with us.

6. What type of _____ works best when you're hanging posters on a wall?

7. Can you believe it's already rained for eight _____ days?

8. A _____ from the school board came to our school meeting to answer questions.

9. Police are not allowed to use _____ force when they arrest a suspect.

10. If you don't understand what the teacher's saying, be _____ and ask for help.

11. The zippers on my sleeves are _____ . They don't really do anything.

12. Adding vivid detail or humor to a story can be done by using

    _____ language.

Name: _____ **Date:** _____

Directions: Use a word from the Word Bank for each section.

Synonyms and Antonyms

Word Bank			
adhesive	alternative	assertive	competitive
comprehensive	consecutive	destructive	excessive
executive	figurative	informative	primitive

Write a synonym for each word or phrase.

1. bold _____

2. in order _____

3. sticky _____

4. thorough _____

Write an antonym for each word or phrase.

5. just for fun _____

6. literal _____

7. constructive _____

8. not enough _____

Write a word that fits each category.

9. judicial, legislative, _____

10. educational, thought-provoking, instructive, _____

11. option, choice, possibility, _____

12. basic, ancient, old-fashioned, _____

Prefixes, Suffixes, and Roots

Name: _____ Date: _____

Directions: Did you know that *gress* and *grad* come from a Latin word that means *step* or *walk*? Use a word from the Word Bank to match each definition.

Word Bank			
aggression	aggressive	congress	digress
egress	grade	gradual	graduate
progress	progression	regress	transgression

1. _____ advance; move or take a **step** forward (*verb*)

2. _____ a series of **steps**, actions, or events that move forward (*noun*)

3. _____ take a **step** back; go back to a previous level or condition (*verb*)

4. _____ wander off topic; take a **step** away from the main subject (*verb*)

5. _____ exit; **step** out of a place (*verb*)

6. _____ the act of **stepping** forward to start a fight or conflict (*noun*)

7. _____ likely to **step** forward and start a fight or conflict (*adjective*)

8. _____ a group of elected people who **step** together to create laws (*noun*)

9. _____ the breaking of a rule or law; the act of "**stepping** over the limit" (*noun*)

10. _____ slow; **step** by **step** (*adjective*)

11. _____ a person's level or **step** (*noun*)

12. _____ finish the last **step** in high school or college (*verb*)

Name: _____ **Date:** _____

Directions: Answer each question in a complete sentence. Remember to turn the question around, and use the bold word in your answer.

1. What are three different types of **adhesives**?

   _____

   _____

2. What does the **executive** branch of our government do?

   _____

   _____

3. Why are **competitive** sports good for kids?

   _____

   _____

4. What's the difference between literal and **figurative** language?

   _____

   _____

5. What are some benefits of using **alternative** energy sources, such as wind and solar power?

   _____

   _____

6. Why do people write letters to their state **representatives**?

   _____

   _____

Analogies

Name: _____ Date: _____

Directions: Use a word from the Word Bank to complete each analogy.

Word Bank			
aggressive	competitive	consecutive	cooperative
decorative	destructive	excessive	executive
figurative	informative	interactive	possessive

1. **willing to share** is to **generous** as **unwilling to share** is to _____

2. **watch** is to **functional** as **bracelet** is to _____

3. **supreme court judge** is to **judicial** as **president** is to _____

4. **test** is to **on your own** as **group project** is to _____

5. **5, 19, 3** is to **random** as **5, 6, 7** is to _____

6. **a hike** is to **recreational** as **a track meet** is to _____

7. **house cat** is to **gentle** as **bobcat** is to _____

8. **storybook** is to **entertaining** as **newspaper article** is to _____

9. **two scoops of ice cream** is to **reasonable** as **six scoops** is to _____

10. **summer breeze** is to **harmless** as **hurricane wind** is to _____

11. **watch TV** is to **passive** as **play a game** is to _____

12. **"My dad is tall."** is to **literal** as **"My dad is a giant."** is to _____

UNIT 10
-ar, -er, and -or Endings

Focus

This week's focus is on multisyllabic words that end with *–ar, –er,* or *–or.* The derivational suffixes *–er* and *–or* change a verb to a noun.

Helpful Hint

Notice that most of the words on this list end with an *r*-controlled vowel (*–ar, –er, –or*) that is pronounced /*er*/. The *–or* suffix changes a verb to a noun and means "a person or object that." For example, an *educator* is someone who *educates*, and a *calculator* is something that *calculates*. The *–ar* ending is used with adjectives (*muscular*) and nouns (*caterpillar*), but is rarely used to name "a type of person or object that."

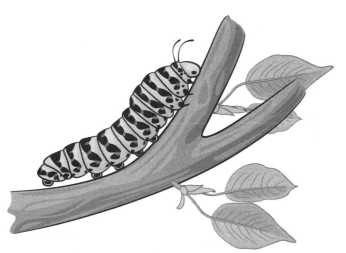

 See the Digital Resources for additional spelling activities.

- alligator
- ambassador
- calculator
- career
- caterpillar
- competitor
- denominator
- educator
- elevator
- engineer
- escalator
- illustrator
- investor
- muscular
- numerator
- particular
- pioneer
- professor
- realtor
- refrigerator

Name: _____ Date: _____

Directions: Use a word from the Word Bank to complete each sentence.

Sentence Completions

Word Bank			
ambassador	career	caterpillar	competitor
denominator	engineer	escalator	investor
muscular	particular	pioneer	realtor

1. We hired a _____ to help us sell our house.

2. Armando is not _____ about his clothes. He'll wear anything as long as it's comfortable.

3. Vanessa has gotten so _____ since she started lifting weights at the gym.

4. The president just appointed a new _____ to the American embassy in Russia.

5. He was a _____ in the field of medical engineering.

6. To reduce a fraction, you have to divide the numerator and _____ by the same number.

7. My little brother loves to ride up and down the _____ whenever we go to the mall.

8. Kennedy is a civil _____ . She will design a new bridge to replace the old, unstable one.

9. Regan is a _____ , but she is always a good sport on the soccer field.

10. Lyanna has a brilliant new invention, but she needs an _____ to help pay for it.

11. Dad's been a detective for 20 years, but he is thinking about starting a new

    _____ .

12. I found a _____ munching on the mulberry leaves in our backyard.

Name: _____ **Date:** _____

Directions: Use a word from the Word Bank for each section.

Word Bank

alligator	ambassador	career	competitor
denominator	educator	elevator	engineer
investor	muscular	particular	refrigerator

Write a synonym for each word.

1. opponent _____

2. choosy _____

3. profession _____

4. strong _____

5. lender _____

Write an antonym for each word.

6. student _____

7. numerator _____

Write a word that fits each category.

8. crocodile, lizard, snake, _____

9. microwave, stove, dishwasher, _____

10. staircase, escalator, pulley system, _____

11. designer, creator, architect, _____

12. diplomat, representative, agent, _____

Synonyms and Antonyms

Prefixes, Suffixes, and Roots

Name: _____ Date: _____

Directions: Did you know that *duc*, *duct*, and *duce* come from a Latin root that means *lead* or *bring*? Use a word from the Word Bank to match each definition.

Word Bank			
abduct	aqueduct	conductor	deduce
duct	education	educator	introduce
produce	productive	reduce	reduction

1. _____ a person who **leads** a band or a train (*noun*)

2. _____ a person who **leads** you to new learning (*noun*)

3. _____ something that **leads** you to new learning (*noun*)

4. _____ kidnap; **lead** a person away from safety (*verb*)

5. _____ **lead** to a lower price or smaller size (*verb*)

6. _____ the act of **leading** to a lower price or smaller size (*noun*)

7. _____ **lead** a conversation with someone new by telling your name (*verb*)

8. _____ make or create; **bring** forth (*verb*)

9. _____ likely to make or create; likely to **bring** forth new items or ideas (*adjective*)

10. _____ a channel or pipe that **brings** water from faraway (*noun*)

11. _____ a tube or channel that **leads** tears out of the eyes or air through a building (*noun*)

12. _____ infer; think about things in a way that **leads** to new conclusions (*verb*)

Name: _____ **Date:** _____

Directions: Your school is hosting a career fair in the cafeteria. Booths are set up around the room, and experts from each field are available to answer questions about their jobs. Write a paragraph that explains which booths you are most excited to visit. Tell why you are interested or curious about these careers. Write a minimum of six sentences and use at least six *–er* or *–or* words.

Word Bank				
actor	ambassador	author	doctor	editor
educator	engineer	farmer	governor	illustrator
investor	janitor	manager	mayor	police officer
private investigator	professor	realtor	school counselor	soldier

_____

_____

_____

_____

_____

_____

_____

_____

_____

_____

_____

_____

_____

_____

_____

_____

_____

Name: _____ **Date:** _____

Analogies

Directions: Use a word from the Word Bank to complete each analogy.

Word Bank			
alligator	ambassador	calculator	competitor
denominator	escalator	illustrator	investor
pioneers	professor	realtor	refrigerator

1. **Massachusetts Bay Colony** is to **Puritans** as **Oregon Trail** is to _____

2. **high school** is to **teacher** as **college** is to _____

3. **measure** is to **ruler** as **add and subtract** is to _____

4. **heat up** is to **oven** as **keep cold** is to _____

5. **top of fraction** is to **numerator** as **bottom of fraction** is to _____

6. **climb up** is to **stairs** as **ride up** is to _____

7. **sell cars** is to **dealer** as **sell houses** is to _____

8. **write words** is to **author** as **draw pictures** is to _____

9. **concert** is to **performer** as **sporting event** is to _____

10. **spend money** is to **consumer** as **invest money** is to _____

11. **ocean** is to **shark** as **swamp** is to _____

12. **spread the news** is to **town crier** as **spread good will** is to _____

28634—180 Days of Spelling and Word Study

UNIT 11
–ation Ending

- admiration
- cancellation
- combination
- conservation
- conversation
- declaration
- expiration
- exploration
- imagination
- information
- inspiration
- invitation
- observation
- organization
- perspiration
- presentation
- preservation
- reservation
- transformation
- transportation

Focus

This week's focus is on multisyllabic words that end with –*ation*. The –*ation* suffix changes a verb to a noun.

Helpful Hint

Notice that all the words on this list end with –*ation*. In some cases, the long *a* serves as a bridge between the verb form of a word and the –*tion* suffix. For example, *relax* becomes *relaxation,* and *present* becomes *presentation*. When the verb ends with silent *e*, the *e* is dropped before the suffix is added (*reserve/reservation, explore/ exploration*).

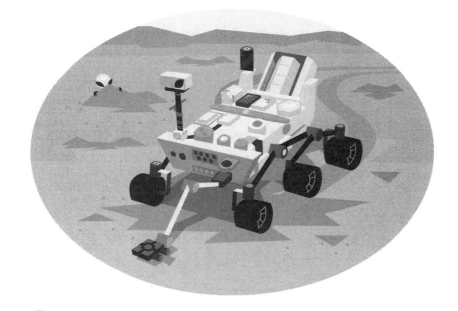

See the Digital Resources for additional spelling activities.

Sentence Completions

Name: _____ Date: _____

Directions: Use a word from the Word Bank to complete each sentence.

Word Bank			
cancellation	conservation	declaration	expiration
exploration	imagination	inspiration	invitation
presentation	preservation	reservation	transformation

1. Can you check the _____ date on the carton of milk? It tastes funny.

2. Aimee underwent a huge _____ when she joined the army. She became much more serious.

3. Thanks to Ballard's underwater _____ , we have learned about deep-sea vents and ridges.

4. Our town's _____ committee hopes to purchase and save 50 more acres of forest land.

5. Tessa is my _____ . She stays positive and never lets her wheelchair slow her down.

6. Did you receive an _____ to Uncle Jack's wedding yet?

7. Due to water _____ policies, we are not allowed to water our lawns during the day.

8. Mara's _____ about manatees was fascinating, but some of the photos made me sad.

9. I used my _____ to convert the garage into a cardboard carnival and arcade.

10. Don't forget to make a _____ at Dobson's. The restaurant is usually busy for dinner.

11. Check the hotel's _____ policy. Will they charge us if we book a room somewhere else?

12. Franklin Roosevelt signed a _____ of war against Japan after the bombing of Pearl Harbor.

Name: _____ **Date:** _____

Directions: Use a word from the Word Bank for each section.

Word Bank			
admiration	cancellation	combination	conservation
conversation	declaration	expiration	inspiration
organization	perspiration	reservation	transformation

Write a synonym for each word or phrase.

1. sweat _____

2. ending date _____

3. announcement _____

Write an antonym for each word or phrase.

4. wasting of resources _____

5. disarray _____

6. disgust _____

7. lack of change _____

8. registration _____

Write a word that fits each category.

9. booking, appointment, hold, _____

10. discussion, dialogue, chat, _____

11. motivator, influence, role model, _____

12. mixture, blend, composite, _____

Synonyms and Antonyms

Prefixes, Suffixes, and Roots

Name: _____ Date: _____

Directions: The *spir* root comes from a Latin word that means *breathe*. The *hal* root comes from a different Latin word that means *breathe*. Use a word from the Word Bank to match each definition.

Word Bank			
aspire	conspiracy	conspire	exhale
expire	inhale	inhaler	inspiration
inspire	perspire	respiration	respiratory

1. _____ **breathe** in (*verb*)

2. _____ **breathe** out (*verb*)

3. _____ a device that people with asthma use to **breathe** in their medicine (*noun*)

4. _____ die or run out; take your last **breath** (*verb*)

5. _____ a single **breath**; something that brings air back into the body (*noun*)

6. _____ describing the system of the body that controls **breathing** (*adjective*)

7. _____ **breathe** life into a person by motivating him or her to do something kind, bold, or creative (*verb*)

8. _____ a motivating thought or idea; something that **breathes** life into you (*noun*)

9. _____ have ambitious hopes or plans; eat, sleep, and **breathe** your goal (*verb*)

10. _____ **breathe** together; devise a devious or unlawful plan with someone (*verb*)

11. _____ a devious or unlawful plan that people **breathe** life into together (*noun*)

12. _____ sweat; "**breathe out**" moisture through your skin's pores (*verb*)

Name: _____ **Date:** _____

Directions: Read each idiom or proverb, and write a sentence explaining its meaning.

1. **Actions** speak louder than words.

    _____

    _____

    _____

2. An ounce of **prevention** is worth a pound of cure.

    _____

    _____

    _____

3. **Imitation** is the sincerest form of flattery.

    _____

    _____

    _____

4. Genius is one percent **inspiration**, ninety-nine percent **perspiration**.

    _____

    _____

    _____

An **idiom** is an expression that is widely used but shouldn't be taken literally. An example is, "It's raining cats and dogs." A **proverb** is a short saying that offers advice. An example is, "Two wrongs don't make a right."

Name: _____ **Date:** _____

Directions: Use a word from the Word Bank to complete each analogy.

Word Bank			
cancellation	conversation	declaration	expiration
information	invitation	observation	organization
perspiration	reservation	transformation	transportation

1. **crying** is to **tears** as **exercise** is to _____

2. **warehouse** is to **storage** as **freight train** is to _____

3. **scale** is to **measurement** as **microscope** is to _____

4. **a little snow** is to **delay** as **a lot of snow** is to _____

5. **911** is to **help** as **search engine** is to _____

6. **court** is to **summons** as **party** is to _____

7. **clean** is to **cleanliness** as **organize** is to _____

8. **doctor's office** is to **appointment** as **restaurant** is to _____

9. **packaged goods** is to **best by date** as **refrigerated goods** is to _____

10. **one topic** is to **discussion** as **many topics** is to _____

11. **announce** is to **announcement** as **declare** is to _____

12. **tadpole to frog** is to **metamorphosis** as **person to superhero** is to _____

UNIT 12

More -tion Endings

Focus

This week's focus is on multisyllabic words that end with –*tion*. The derivational suffix –*tion* changes a verb to a noun.

Helpful Hint

Notice that all the words on this list end with –*tion*. The –*tion* suffix changes a verb to a noun. When a verb ends with –*fy* or –*ply*, the *y* changes to *i*, and the –*cation* suffix is added (*multiply/multiplication, apply/application, notify/notification, qualify/qualification*). When a verb ends with –*olve*, the –*ve* is replaced by –*ution* (*revolve/revolution, solve/solution, resolve/resolution*).

> abbreviation
> application
> communication
> congratulations
> constitution
> decoration
> evaporation
> inauguration
> institution
> investigation
> legislation
> multiplication
> notification
> participation
> qualifications
> recreation
> resolution
> revolution
> solution
> unification

🔍 See the Digital Resources for additional spelling activities.

Sentence Completions

Name: _____ **Date:** _____

Directions: Use a word from the Word Bank to complete each sentence.

Word Bank			
application	constitution	decoration	inauguration
institution	investigation	legislation	notification
recreation	resolution	Revolution	unification

1. My New Year's _____ is to get more fresh air and exercise.

2. Hopefully, Congress will pass _____ that makes it easier to catch cyber criminals.

3. Did you receive a _____ on your phone about football try-outs?

4. During the _____ , the president gets sworn into office on the steps of the Capitol.

5. My sister filled out a job _____ at the grocery store. She wants to be a cashier.

6. The teen center has a large _____ area where you can play pool, watch movies, or dance.

7. Pennsylvania Hospital is the oldest medical _____ in the United States. It opened in 1751.

8. The _____ of North and South Vietnam took place in 1975. They became one country.

9. Our classroom _____ governs how we behave.

10. A _____ for the Halloween dance fell off the ceiling in the middle of my favorite song.

11. The American _____ started with battles in Lexington and Concord.

12. I hope we'll get some answers when the police finish their _____ .

28634—180 Days of Spelling and Word Study   © *Shell Education*

Synonyms and Antonyms

Name: _____ **Date:** _____

Directions: Use a word from the Word Bank for each section.

Word Bank

congratulations	decorations	evaporation	institution
investigation	legislation	multiplication	notification
qualification	recreation	revolution	solution

Write a synonym for each word.

1. fun _____
2. probe _____

Write an antonym for each word.

3. condolences _____
4. division _____
5. condensation _____
6. problem _____

Write a word that fits each category.

7. laws, bills, statutes, _____
8. refreshments, games, goody bags, _____
9. organization, company, business, _____
10. skill, experience, accomplishment, _____
11. revolt, uprising, rebellion, _____
12. flyer, notice, announcement, _____

Name: _____ **Date:** _____

Directions: Did you know that *grat* and *grac* come from a Latin word that means *pleasing* or *thankful*? Use a word from the Word Bank to match each definition.

Word Bank			
congratulate	congratulations	disgrace	grace
graceful	gracious	grateful	gratification
gratifying	gratitude	gratuity	ungrateful

1. _____ **thankful** (*adjective*)

2. _____ not **thankful** (*adjective*)

3. _____ **thankfulness** (*noun*)

4. _____ **pleasing** or satisfying (*adjective*)

5. _____ the act of **pleasing** or satisfying a person (*noun*)

6. _____ a tip; money that shows you're **pleased** with the service you've received (*noun*)

7. _____ express **pleasure** to a person for her success or good fortune (*verb*)

8. _____ expressions of **pleasure** when a person succeeds or has good fortune (*noun*)

9. _____ charm or ease of movement; a **pleasing** trait or mannerism (*noun*)

10. _____ able to move with ease, in a smooth and **pleasing** way (*adjective*)

11. _____ **pleasant**, like a good host; exhibiting courtesy and kindness (*adjective*)

12. _____ bring shame to oneself; cause others to look with **displeasure** (*verb*)

Name: _____ **Date:** _____

Directions: Answer each question in a complete sentence. Remember to turn the question around, and use the bold word in your answer.

1. What are some common New Year's **resolutions**?

   _____

   _____

2. Why should students be graded on their class **participation**?

   _____

   _____

3. When might people offer others **congratulations**?

   _____

   _____

4. Why is the presidential **inauguration** an important occasion?

   _____

   _____

5. What are some types of **recreation** people enjoy?

   _____

   _____

6. What are some **qualifications** that a soccer coach should have?

   _____

   _____

Turn the Question Around

Name: _____ Date: _____

Analogies

Directions: Use a word from the Word Bank to complete each analogy.

Word Bank

abbreviation	communication	congratulations	decoration
evaporation	inauguration	investigation	legislation
multiplication	qualifications	recreation	resolution

1. **gas to liquid** is to **condensation** as **liquid to gas** is to _____

2. **punch** is to **refreshment** as **balloons** is to _____

3. **Connecticut** is to **word** as **CT** is to _____

4. **shopping list** is to **groceries** as **résumé** is to _____

5. **funeral** is to **condolences** as **wedding** is to _____

6. **birthday** is to **wish** as **New Year's Eve** is to _____

7. **Supreme Court** is to **rulings** as **Congress** is to _____

8. **swimming** is to **movement** as **talking** is to _____

9. **November** is to **election** as **January** is to _____

10. **office building** is to **work** as **park** is to _____

11. **12 ÷ 4** is to **division** as **12 x 4** is to _____

12. **scientists** is to **research** as **detectives** is to _____

UNIT 13

–sion Ending

Focus

This week's focus is on multisyllabic words that end with –sion. The derivational suffix –sion changes a verb to a noun.

Helpful Hint

Notice that all the words on this list end with –sion. The –sion suffix changes a verb to a noun. For example, *depress* becomes *depression*, and *supervise* becomes *supervision*. Drop the silent *e* before adding a –sion suffix. Some roots change in predictable ways: *mit* becomes *mis* (*commit/commission, transmit/transmission*), and –*d* or –*de* endings drop off (*comprehend/comprehension, suspend/suspension, persuade/persuasion, provide/provisions*).

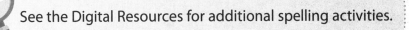
See the Digital Resources for additional spelling activities.

- aggression
- apprehension
- commission
- comprehension
- concessions
- concussion
- depression
- diversion
- excursion
- illusion
- incision
- obsession
- persuasion
- precision
- procession
- progression
- provisions
- supervision
- suspension
- television

Name: _____ **Date:** _____

Directions: Use a word from the Word Bank to complete each sentence.

Word Bank			
aggression	apprehension	commission	diversion
excursion	illusion	obsession	persuasion
precision	procession	progression	suspension

1. Alexis was filled with _____ when she stepped on the stage to give her speech.

2. Babies follow a natural _____ when they learn to walk.

3. Dad removed the splinter from Jade's foot with the _____ of a surgeon.

4. Tao used his powers of _____ to convince Grandpa he needed another toy.

5. The inaugural _____ starts on the steps of the Capitol and ends at the White House.

6. Frankie's _____ with stuffed animals is getting out of hand. The entire house is covered with them!

7. The student received a two-day _____ for bad choices.

8. Shooting baskets or kicking a soccer ball are great ways to get out your _____ .

9. Large mirrors create an _____ by tricking the mind into thinking a room is much bigger.

10. We took an _____ to the ice cream factory while on vacation.

11. My sister and I created a _____ for the crying baby by making funny faces.

12. My aunt is a realtor. She earns a _____ every time she sells a house.

Name: _____ **Date:** _____

Directions: Use a word from the Word Bank for each section.

Word Bank			
aggression	apprehension	commission	concessions
depression	diversion	excursion	incision
obsession	procession	provisions	supervision

Write a synonym for each word or phrase.

1. surgical cut _____

2. parade _____

3. day trip _____

4. anxiety _____

Write an antonym for each word or phrase.

5. negligence _____

6. gentleness _____

7. happiness _____

8. lack of interest _____

Write a word that fits each category.

9. food, supplies, rations, _____

10. entertainment, distraction, attention-grabber, _____

11. tips, gratuity, bonus, _____

12. snacks, refreshments, souvenirs, _____

Name: _____ **Date:** _____

Directions: Did you know that *cis and cide* come from a Latin word that means *cut off* or *kill*? Use a word from the Word Bank to match each definition.

Word Bank			
concise	decide	decision	excise
imprecise	incision	incisor	indecisive
pesticide	precise	precision	scissors

1. _____ a tooth that is used for **cutting** into food (*noun*)

2. _____ a surgical **cut** made into skin (*noun*)

3. _____ a sharp tool that is used for **cutting** paper (*noun*)

4. _____ remove a tumor or growth by **cutting** it out of the body (*verb*)

5. _____ make a final choice; **cut off** thinking about something (*verb*)

6. _____ a final choice; the **cutting off** of thinking about a topic (*noun*)

7. _____ unable to make a final choice or **cut off** thinking about something (*adjective*)

8. _____ brief and to the point; all the extra details have been **cut off** (*adjective*)

9. _____ exact and accurate; **cut** just right (*adjective*)

10. _____ not exact and accurate; not **cut** right (*adjective*)

11. _____ the quality of being exact and accurate; the quality of being **cut** just right (*noun*)

12. _____ a chemical that is used to **kill** insects or garden pests (*noun*)

Name: _____ **Date:** _____

Directions: You have been selected to participate in a television survey. The Nielsen Company wants to know more about the TV viewing habits of young people. Write a paragraph that describes the types of shows you enjoy and the types of shows you avoid. Write at least six sentences and use a minimum of six –*sion* words (or forms of the words).

Word Bank				
apprehension	collision	comprehension	concussion	decision
discussion	diversion	excursion	expression	fashion
illusion	mansion	obsession	occasion	passion
persuasion	precision	profession	supervision	television

_____
_____
_____
_____
_____
_____
_____
_____
_____
_____
_____
_____
_____
_____
_____
_____
_____
_____

Name: _____ Date:_____

Directions: Use a word from the Word Bank to complete each analogy.

Analogies

Word Bank			
commission	comprehension	concessions	concussion
depression	excursion	incision	precision
procession	provisions	suspension	television

1. **waiter** is to **tips** as **salesperson** is to _____

2. **sports field** is to **snacks** as **state fair** is to _____

3. **interactive** is to **computer** as **passive** is to _____

4. **joy** is to **elation** as **sadness** is to _____

5. **pads** is to **bruises** as **helmet** is to _____

6. **needle** is to **stitches** as **scalpel** is to _____

7. **expel** is to **expulsion** as **suspend** is to _____

8. **long journey** is to **trek** as **short trip** is to _____

9. **pack for school** is to **lunch** as **pack for campout** is to _____

10. **cars on the highway** is to **traffic** as **cars at a funeral** is to _____

11. **read smoothly** is to **fluency** as **read with understanding** is to _____

12. **preschool teacher** is to **patience** as **brain surgeon** is to _____

UNIT 14
–able Ending

Focus

This week's focus is on multisyllabic words that end with –able. The derivational suffix –able changes a verb to an adjective.

Helpful Hint

Notice that all the words on this list end with –able. The –able suffix changes a verb to an adjective and means "able to." For example, something *respectable* is *able to be respected*, and people are *able to compare* things that are *comparable*. We drop the silent *e* before we add an –able suffix, unless we need to keep the *g* or *c* soft (*manageable*, *noticeable*).

🔍 See the Digital Resources for additional spelling activities.

> **charitable**
> **comfortable**
> **comparable**
> **considerable**
> **inevitable**
> **irritable**
> **knowledgeable**
> **manageable**
> **memorable**
> **noticeable**
> **perishable**
> **probable**
> **reasonable**
> **remarkable**
> **respectable**
> **unavoidable**
> **unbelievable**
> **undependable**
> **variables**
> **vulnerable**

Sentence Completions

Name: _____ **Date:** _____

Directions: Use a word from the Word Bank to complete each sentence.

Word Bank			
charitable	comfortable	comparable	inevitable
irritable	manageable	noticeable	perishable
probable	reasonable	variables	vulnerable

1. Do you think it's _____ to charge $10 per hour for babysitting?

2. Put the _____ items in the refrigerator. Everything else can go in the pantry.

3. Is the stain on my shirt _____ ? I tried to cover it with a necklace.

4. The hotels we stayed at were _____ . They were both clean and offered free breakfasts.

5. All brothers and sisters fight sometimes. Disagreements are _____ .

6. Mom's looking for a new job closer to home. She needs a commute that's more _____ .

7. Make yourself _____ on the couch while I get us some cold drinks and snacks.

8. It is _____ that we will have to stay inside today since there are thunderstorms in the area.

9. Every year, we raise money for a _____ cause in the community.

10. Janice gets _____ and snaps at people when she's overtired.

11. Ravi felt scared and _____ when his parents left him alone for an hour at the baseball field.

12. You must consider a lot of _____ , such as cost and location, when you rent an apartment.

Name: _____ **Date:** _____

Directions: Use a word from the Word Bank for each section.

Word Bank			
charitable	comfortable	comparable	inevitable
irritable	knowledgeable	noticeable	probable
remarkable	unbelievable	undependable	vulnerable

Write a synonym for each word or phrase.

1. cranky _____
2. unavoidable _____
3. in danger _____
4. similar _____

Write an antonym for each word.

5. stingy _____
6. unlikely _____
7. ignorant _____
8. reliable _____

Write a word that fits each category.

9. obvious, apparent, easy to see, _____
10. relaxed, cozy, snug, _____
11. amazing, impressive, outstanding, _____
12. unthinkable, incredible, unimaginable, _____

Name: _____ Date: _____

Directions: Did you know that *pend* comes from a Latin word that means *hang* or *weigh*? Use a word from the Word Bank to match each definition.

Word Bank

depend	dependable	dependent	impending
independent	pendant	pending	pendulum
suspend	suspenders	suspension	undependable

1. _____ something that **hangs** and swings back and forth, such as a **weight** on a clock (*noun*)

2. _____ a piece of jewelry that **hangs** from a chain around the neck (*noun*)

3. _____ rely on someone; **weigh** him or her down with responsibility (*verb*)

4. _____ reliable; able to handle the **weight** of someone or something (*adjective*)

5. _____ not reliable; not able to handle the **weight** of someone or something (*adjective*)

6. _____ **hanging** on someone or something for support or survival (*adjective*)

7. _____ able to stand alone; not **hanging** on someone or something else (*adjective*)

8. _____ **hang** from the ceiling or in the air, such as a light fixture or circus performer (*verb*)

9. _____ shoulder straps that keep a person's pants **hanging** around the waist (*noun*)

10. _____ a period of time when a student is left **hanging**, unable to attend school because of misbehavior (*noun*)

11. _____ not decided or resolved yet; "**hanging** in the balance" (*adjective*)

12. _____ about to happen; **hanging** in the distance (*adjective*)

Prefixes, Suffixes, and Roots

Name: _____ Date: _____

Directions: Answer each question in a complete sentence. Remember to turn the question around, and use the bold word in your answer.

1. Why are infants more **vulnerable** to infections than older children?

    _____

    _____

2. Where are you most **comfortable** doing homework?

    _____

    _____

3. How can you make a stain on your shirt less **noticeable**?

    _____

    _____

4. Why is it **reasonable** to expect children to walk less than a mile to school?

    _____

    _____

5. Why is teaching a **respectable** job?

    _____

    _____

6. What is the most **memorable** day you've spent with your family?

    _____

    _____

Turn the Question Around

Analogies

Name: _____ Date: _____

Directions: Use a word from the Word Bank to complete each analogy.

Word Bank			
charitable	comfortable	comparable	inevitable
irritable	memorable	noticeable	perishable
probable	reasonable	unbelievable	vulnerable

1. **too hot** is to **uncomfortable** as **just right** is to _____

2. **pimple on scalp** is to **hidden** as **pimple on nose** is to _____

3. **can of soup** is to **nonperishable** as **carton of milk** is to _____

4. **flying birds** is to **believable** as **flying dogs** is to _____

5. **locked car** is to **safe** as **unlocked car** is to _____

6. **birthday celebration** is to **optional** as **getting older** is to _____

7. **cold medicines** is to **drowsy** as **itchy bug bites** is to _____

8. **recipient** is to **grateful** as **donor** is to _____

9. **typical day** is to **forgettable** as **day with friends** is to _____

10. **nickel and penny** is to **different** as **nickel and five pennies** is to _____

11. **snow in Hawaii** is to **unlikely** as **snow in New York** is to _____

12. **six slices of pizza** is to **excessive** as **two slices of pizza** is to _____

UNIT 15

–ible Ending

Focus

This week's focus is on multisyllabic words that end with –ible. The derivational suffix –ible changes a verb to an adjective.

Helpful Hint

Notice that all the words on this list end with –ible. The –ible suffix is found at the end of adjectives and means *able to*. It is less common than –able and is usually found after roots that cannot stand alone (*feas·ible*, *elig·ible*). Many of the words on this list contain a variant of the *in–* prefix, which means *not* (*in·credible*, *ir·reversible*, *im·possible*, *il·legible*).

➤ compatible
➤ convertible
➤ distractible
➤ divisible
➤ eligible
➤ feasible
➤ illegible
➤ impossible
➤ incredible
➤ indelible
➤ indestructible
➤ indivisible
➤ infallible
➤ inflexible
➤ invincible
➤ invisible
➤ irresistible
➤ irreversible
➤ responsible
➤ reversible

See the Digital Resources for additional spelling activities.

Name: _____ **Date:** _____

Directions: Use a word from the Word Bank to complete each sentence.

Sentence Completions

Word Bank			
compatible	convertible	distractible	feasible
illegible	incredible	indelible	indestructible
infallible	invisible	irresistible	irreversible

1. No one is _____ . Everyone makes mistakes sometimes.

2. It's not _____ to get home from work, make dinner, and get to practice on time.

3. They need to invent _____ cellphones that can withstand any disaster.

4. Grandpa loves to drive around in his _____ when the weather's nice.

5. Tremaine captured _____ photos of the volcano erupting.

6. Mrs. Nguyen left an _____ mark on her students' hearts. They will never forget her.

7. The accident caused _____ damage to Layla's leg. Doctors couldn't repair it.

8. I don't think my older brother and his girlfriend are _____ since they argue constantly.

9. Parker has to do his homework in a quiet, empty room because he's so _____ .

10. Carbon monoxide is an _____ , odorless gas that is hard to detect.

11. Sometimes Mom gets an _____ urge to go out for ice cream.

12. Dad's handwriting is so _____ that he can't even read it!

28634—180 Days of Spelling and Word Study © *Shell Education*

Name: _____ **Date:** _____

Directions: Use a word from the Word Bank for each section.

Word Bank

compatible	convertible	distractible	eligible
feasible	illegible	incredible	indelible
indestructible	infallible	invisible	irresistible

Write a synonym for each word.

1. unseeable _____

2. shocking _____

3. perfect _____

4. qualified _____

Write an antonym for each word or phrase.

5. neatly written _____

6. erasable _____

7. focused _____

8. flimsy _____

Write a word that fits each category.

9. practical, possible, achievable, _____

10. harmonious, agreeable, able to get along, _____

11. tempting, enticing, overpowering, _____

12. minivan, sedan, compact, _____

Synonyms and Antonyms

Prefixes, Suffixes, and Roots

Name: _____ **Date:** _____

Directions: Did you know that *flect* and *flex* come from a Latin word that means *bend*? Use a word from the Word Bank to match each definition.

Word Bank			
deflect	flex	flexibility	flexible
inflection	inflexible	reflect	reflection
reflective	reflector	reflex	

1. _____ **bend**, such as the muscles in one's arm (*verb*)

2. _____ able to **bend** easily (*adjective*)

3. _____ the quality of being able to **bend** easily (*noun*)

4. _____ rigid; not able to **bend** easily (*adjective*)

5. _____ **bend** or push something so it changes direction (*verb*)

6. _____ cause light rays to **bend** back, such as an image in a mirror (*verb*)

7. _____ the **bending** of light rays in a mirror or pane of glass (*noun*)

8. _____ plastic that **bends** light, making it easier for a bike to be seen in the dark (*noun*)

9. _____ a movement that happens without conscious thought, such as the **bending** of a knee that is tapped (*noun*)

10. _____ the rise and fall of a voice; the way a person's voice **bends** when he or she talks (*verb*)

11. _____ thoughtful; tending to **bend** ideas over and over in one's mind (*adjective*)

Name: _____   Date: _____

Directions: Answer each question in a complete sentence. Remember to turn the question around, and use the bold word in your answer.

1. Why is the word **indivisible** used in the Pledge of Allegiance?

    _____

    _____

2. At what age are American citizens **eligible** to run for president?

    _____

    _____

3. What are three numbers that are **divisible** by nine?

    _____

    _____

4. Why should **indelible** markers be kept away from young children?

    _____

    _____

5. Why isn't it **feasible** to move furniture into a house all by yourself?

    _____

    _____

6. Are all phone chargers **compatible**? Explain.

    _____

    _____

Analogies

Name: _____ **Date:** _____

Directions: Use a word from the Word Bank to complete each analogy.

Word Bank			
compatible	convertible	distractible	illegible
impossible	incredible	indelible	inflexible
invincible	invisible	responsible	reversible

1. **neat handwriting** is to **legible** as **messy scrawl** is to _____

2. **live to be 100** is to **feasible** as **live to be 1,000** is to _____

3. **washable marker** is to **erasable** as **permanent marker** is to _____

4. **immovable roof** is to **sedan** as **removable roof** is to _____

5. **humans** is to **destructible** as **gods** is to _____

6. **aluminum foil** is to **flexible** as **steel beam** is to _____

7. **engaged learner** is to **focused** as **bored student** is to _____

8. **losing homework** is to **careless** as **turning in homework** is to _____

9. **wood to ashes** is to **irreversible** as **water to ice** is to _____

10. **enemies** is to **hostile** as **friends** is to _____

11. **drinking fountain** is to **unimpressive** as **Niagara Falls** is to _____

12. **light waves** is to **visible** as **radio waves** is to _____

UNIT 16
–ic Ending

Focus

This week's focus is on multisyllabic words that end with –ic. The derivational suffix –ic can change a noun to an adjective.

Helpful Hint

Notice that all the words on this list end with –ic. The –ic suffix changes a noun to an adjective (*democracy/democratic, drama/dramatic, majesty/majestic*). Some –ic words can be used as nouns as well (*antibiotic, epidemic*).

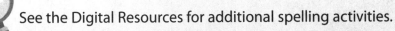
See the Digital Resources for additional spelling activities.

WEEK 16

- academic
- aerobic
- Antarctic
- antibiotic
- Arctic
- authentic
- automatic
- ceramic
- democratic
- domestic
- dramatic
- economics
- energetic
- epidemic
- exotic
- majestic
- pathetic
- patriotic
- sympathetic
- traumatic

Name: _____ **Date:** _____

Directions: Use a word from the Word Bank to complete each sentence.

Word Bank			
academic	aerobic	antibiotic	Arctic
authentic	automatic	democratic	domestic
economics	epidemic	exotic	sympathetic

1. My uncle travels to _____ places to photograph beautiful and unusual creatures.

2. We follow a _____ process when we select our local and national leaders.

3. My cousin is studying _____ in college so he can learn how to run his own business.

4. People were so _____ when Grandma died. We appreciated their cards and kind words.

5. Parts of the _____ Circle stay dark for 24 hours a day during the winter months.

6. Exercise that increases blood flow to your whole body and makes you breathe faster is

   called _____ .

7. We brought the painting to an art dealer to see if it was _____ or just a copy.

8. My favorite _____ subject at school is social studies.

9. I wish we had an _____ garage door opener so we wouldn't have to open it by hand.

10. World leaders tried to contain the Ebola _____ before it spread to more countries.

11. If you skip doses of the _____ , it won't work as well and you'll probably get sick again.

12. My little brother helps with _____ chores. He throws the dirty laundry downstairs.

Name: _____ **Date:** _____

Directions: Use a word from the Word Bank for each section.

Word Bank			
antibiotic	Arctic	authentic	automatic
domestic	dramatic	energetic	epidemic
exotic	majestic	pathetic	traumatic

Write a synonym for each word or phrase.

1. devastating _____

2. pitiful _____

3. excitedly different _____

4. without conscious thought _____

Write an antonym for each word.

5. fake _____

6. sluggish _____

7. international _____

8. soothing _____

Write a word that fits each category.

9. cough syrup, pain reliever, antihistamine, _____

10. Pacific, Atlantic, Indian, _____

11. grand, magnificent, impressive, _____

12. outbreak, pandemic, plague, _____

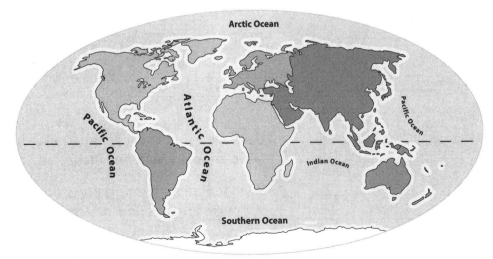

Prefixes, Suffixes, and Roots

Name: _____ Date: _____

Directions: The root *path* comes from a Greek word that means *feeling*. *Pass* comes from a Latin word that means *suffer* or *feel*. Use a word from the Word Bank to match each definition.

Word Bank			
apathy	compassion	compassionate	empathetic
empathize	empathy	passion	passionate
pathetic	sympathetic	sympathize	sympathy

1. _____ understand and share the **feelings** of another person (*verb*)

2. _____ the ability to understand and share another person's **feelings** (*noun*)

3. _____ able to share and understand another person's **feelings** (*adjective*)

4. _____ express **feelings** of sorrow or pity for another person's loss (*verb*)

5. _____ the **expression** of sorrow or pity for another person's loss (*noun*)

6. _____ able to express **feelings** of sorrow or pity for another person's loss (*adjective*)

7. _____ indifference; a lack of **feeling** (*noun*)

8. _____ causing **emotions** of pity or sadness (*adjective*)

9. _____ strong, barely controlled **emotion** (*noun*)

10. _____ able to feel strong **emotion** (*adjective*)

11. _____ a deep sadness and **expression** of kindness toward another's suffering (*noun*)

12. _____ able to **feel** sadness and express kindness toward others who are suffering (*adjective*)

Name: _____   **Date:** _____

Directions: Answer each question in a complete sentence. Remember to turn the question around, and use the bold word in your answer.

1. What are three types of **aerobic** exercise?

    _____

    _____

2. What is your favorite **patriotic** song?

    _____

    _____

3. Why should children help with **domestic** chores, such as dishes and laundry?

    _____

    _____

4. Why is it hard to find **exotic** fruits and vegetables in your neighborhood grocery store?

    _____

    _____

5. Why do people need prescriptions to get **antibiotics**?

    _____

    _____

6. How are leaders selected in a **democratic** country?

    _____

    _____

Turn the Question Around

Analogies

Name: _____   Date: _____

Directions: Use a word from the Word Bank to complete each analogy.

Word Bank			
academic	aerobic	Antarctic	antibiotic
Arctic	ceramic	democratic	domestic
energetic	epidemic	exotic	patriotic

1. **North Pole** is to **Arctic** as **South Pole** is to _____

2. **self-appointed leader** is to **autocratic** as **elected leader** is to _____

3. **yoga** is to **strength training** as **jogging** is to _____

4. **community** is to **outbreak** as **region** is to _____

5. **gym class** is to **athletic** as **math class** is to _____

6. **faucet** is to **metal** as **toilet** is to _____

7. **overtired** is to **sluggish** as **well-rested** is to _____

8. **flight to Europe** is to **international** as **flight to Florida** is to _____

9. **cold** is to **rest and fluids** as **strep throat** is to _____

10. **penguin** is to **Antarctic** as **polar bear** is to _____

11. **Christmas wreath** is to **festive** as **American flag** is to _____

12. **robins and blue jays** is to **native** as **macaws and cockatoos** is to _____

28634—180 Days of Spelling and Word Study

UNIT 17
–al Ending

- alphabetical
- carnival
- collateral
- critical
- emotional
- horizontal
- hysterical
- intentional
- international
- interval
- literal
- maternal
- nocturnal
- numeral
- paternal
- perpetual
- practical
- rehearsal
- terminal
- universal

Focus

This week's focus is on multisyllabic words that end with –al. The –al ending is found in nouns and adjectives. The derivational suffix –al can change a noun to an adjective.

Helpful Hint

Notice that all the words on this list end with –al. The –al ending is used with adjectives (*international*, *maternal*) and nouns (*interval*, *terminal*). Nouns that end with –tion become adjectives when the –al suffix is added (*nation/national*, *emotion/emotional*). Many nouns can be changed into adverbs by adding –al, plus –ly (*magic/magically*, *nature/naturally*, *practice/practically*).

See the Digital Resources for additional spelling activities.

Sentence Completions

Name: _____   Date:_____

Directions: Use a word from the Word Bank to complete each sentence.

Word Bank			
alphabetical	collateral	critical	emotional
hysterical	intentional	interval	maternal
numeral	perpetual	rehearsal	terminal

1. A parking shuttle dropped us off in front of the airport _____ , then we walked to Gate 12.

2. My _____ grandmother was born in Greece, but my dad's mom was born in the United States.

3. We have one more _____ before opening night!

4. Pedro's arms and legs are in _____ motion. He never sits still!

5. Two victims were flown to the hospital, and they were listed in

    _____ condition.

6. Ashley said I could borrow her bike, but she's holding onto my rollerblades as

    _____ .

7. During _____ training in gym, we alternate between sprinting and walking.

8. The _____ eight fell off our mailbox, so now no one can tell which house is ours.

9. I don't know if Jasmine stepped on Max's toy accidentally or if it was

    _____ .

10. Raul's performance at the talent show was _____ . I couldn't stop laughing!

11. All the books are arranged on the shelves in _____ order by author.

12. Mom always gets _____ when she says goodbye to us on the first day of school.

Name: _____   **Date:** _____

Directions: Use a word from the Word Bank for each section.

Word Bank			
carnival	critical	emotional	horizontal
hysterical	intentional	interval	literal
perpetual	practical	rehearsal	universal

Write a synonym for each word or phrase.

1. very funny _____

2. nonstop _____

3. worldwide _____

4. very important _____

Write an antonym for each word.

5. accidental _____

6. figurative _____

7. vertical _____

8. calm _____

Write a word that fits each category.

9. fair, festival, jamboree, _____

10. break, pause, gap, _____

11. useful, sensible, real-world, _____

12. practice, dry run, preview, _____

Name: _____ Date: _____

Directions: Did you know that the roots *mater* and *matri* comes from a Latin word that means *mother*? The roots *pater* and *patri* come from a Latin word that means *father*. Use a word from the Word Bank to match each definition.

Word Bank			
maternal	maternity	matriarch	matrimony
matron	paternal	paternity	patriarch
patriot	patriotic	patron	

1. _____ caring or nurturing, like a **mom**; related on **Mom's** side of the family (*adjective*)

2. _____ the quality or state of being a **mom** (*noun*)

3. _____ the **mom** figure, or female head of a family (*noun*)

4. _____ a married woman, often a woman who is or will soon become a **mom** (*noun*)

5. _____ the state of being married (*noun*)

6. _____ caring or nurturing, like a **dad**; related on **Dad's** side of the family (*adjective*)

7. _____ **father**hood (*noun*)

8. _____ the **dad** figure, or male head of a family (*noun*)

9. _____ a person who gives money or support to a cause, such as a generous **dad** (*noun*)

10. _____ someone who loves his or her country or **father**land (*noun*)

11. _____ showing love and support for one's country or **father**land (*adjective*)

Name: _____ Date: _____

Directions: Answer each question in a complete sentence. Remember to turn the question around, and use the bold word in your answer.

1. Why do most teenagers like fast **carnival** rides?

    _____

    _____

2. How does a pitcher cause an **intentional** walk in baseball?

    _____

    _____

3. What could you find in an airport **terminal**?

    _____

    _____

4. Why do banks require **collateral** when they give people loans?

    _____

    _____

5. What is a dress **rehearsal**?

    _____

    _____

6. What is the **universal** sign for choking?

    _____

    _____

Analogies

Name: _____ **Date:** _____

Directions: Use a word from the Word Bank to complete each analogy.

Word Bank			
carnival	horizontal	hysterical	intentional
international	literal	nocturnal	numeral
paternal	perpetual	rehearsal	universal

1. **mother** is to **maternal** as **father** is to _____

2. **bird** is to **diurnal** as **bat** is to _____

3. **actor** is to **movie** as **clown** is to _____

4. **game** is to **practice** as **performance** is to _____

5. **"My room is a pigsty."** is to **figurative** as **"My room is messy."** is to _____

6. **boring** is to **mind-numbing** as **funny** is to _____

7. **flight to New York** is to **domestic** as **flight to Japan** is to _____

8. **longitude** is to **vertical** as **latitude** is to _____

9. **bump into someone** is to **accidental** as **punch someone** is to _____

10. **people shake hands** is to **regional** as **people breathe air** is to _____

11. **A** is to **letter** as **1** is to _____

12. **carousel's spinning** is to **intermittent** as **Earth's spinning** is to _____

UNIT 18

–ant and –ance Endings

Focus

This week's focus is on multisyllabic words that end with –ant, –ance, or –ancy. The –ant suffix signifies a noun or adjective. When –ant changes to –ance or –ancy, it changes an adjective to a noun.

Helpful Hint

Notice that all the words on this list end with –ant or –ance. The –ant ending is usually used with adjectives (defiant, significant). Adjectives that end with –ant become nouns when –ant is changed to –ance (arrogant/arrogance, ignorant/ignorance) or –ancy (pregnant/pregnancy, vacant/vacancy).

- ➤ abundant
- ➤ appliance
- ➤ arrogance
- ➤ attendance
- ➤ buoyancy
- ➤ defiant
- ➤ discrepancy
- ➤ endurance
- ➤ extravagant
- ➤ ignorant
- ➤ insurance
- ➤ maintenance
- ➤ observant
- ➤ occupancy
- ➤ pregnancy
- ➤ redundant
- ➤ reluctant
- ➤ resistant
- ➤ significant
- ➤ vacancy

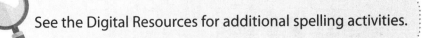

See the Digital Resources for additional spelling activities.

Sentence Completions

Name: _____ Date: _____

Directions: Use a word from the Word Bank to complete each sentence.

Word Bank			
abundant	arrogance	defiant	discrepancy
insurance	maintenance	occupancy	redundant
reluctant	resistant	significant	vacancy

1. Every word in a poem is _____ because it was carefully selected for its meaning.

2. There was a _____ between the price tag and the amount that rang up on the cash register.

3. Some infections have grown _____ to antibiotics, so new medicines are being developed.

4. If there's no _____ at the hotel, we might have to sleep in our car!

5. I was _____ to try out for the school soccer team, but Jack convinced me to do it.

6. Dad's bringing our car to the garage Saturday for routine _____ .

7. We'll need a bigger room for the party. The maximum _____ at this place is 40 guests.

8. We have an _____ supply of paper and pencils, but we are starting to run out of glue sticks.

9. I can't believe Scott's _____ ! He never stops bragging about how smart he is.

10. Hopefully, Caroline's _____ will pay for a new car since her car got totaled in the accident.

11. Three students were openly _____ and refused to do anything the substitute said.

12. Is it _____ to say that my aunt gave birth to *two* twins?

Name: _____ **Date:** _____

Directions: Use a word from the Word Bank for each section.

Word Bank

abundant	arrogance	buoyancy	defiant
discrepancy	endurance	extravagant	ignorant
insurance	maintenance	redundant	reluctant

Write a synonym for each word or phrase.

1. stamina _____

2. upkeep _____

3. plentiful _____

4. ability to float _____

Write an antonym for each word.

5. knowledgeable _____

6. obedient _____

7. humility _____

8. eager _____

Write a word that fits each category.

9. expensive, wasteful, lavish, _____

10. difference, mismatch, lack of consistency, _____

11. coverage, protection, security, _____

12. repetitive, extra, not necessary, _____

Prefixes, Suffixes, and Roots

Name: _____ **Date:** _____

Directions: Did you know that the root *sign* comes from a Latin word that means *sign, mark,* or *indication*? Use a word from the Word Bank to match each definition.

Word Bank			
assign	assignment	consign	designate
designer	insignificant	resign	sign
signal	signature	significance	significant

1. _____ **mark** a form with your name; or, use hand gestures to **indicate** meaning (*verb*)

2. _____ a person's name, **marked** on paper (*noun*)

3. _____ a gesture or blinking light that **indicates** something needs attention (*noun*)

4. _____ noteworthy; **indicating** importance (*adjective*)

5. _____ not noteworthy; not **indicating** importance (*adjective*)

6. _____ importance; the quality or **indication** of deeper meaning (*noun*)

7. _____ a person who creates or **marks out** plans for new clothes or websites (*noun*)

8. _____ give a student or employee a task; **indicate** a job that needs to be done (*verb*)

9. _____ a job or task that has been **marked** for a particular person (*noun*)

10. _____ quit a job; **indicate** that you no longer wish to be an employee (*verb*)

11. _____ offer your clothes or household items to a business to resell them; **mark** your items for resale (*verb*)

12. _____ **mark** someone or something for a special purpose, such as an emergency contact or the heir of a will (*verb*)

Name: _____   **Date:** _____

Directions: Read each idiom or proverb, and write a sentence explaining its meaning.

1. **Ignorance** is bliss.

   _____

   _____

   _____

2. within striking **distance**

   _____

   _____

   _____

3. the **elephant** in the room

   _____

   _____

   _____

4. A picture is worth a **thousand** words.

   _____

   _____

   _____

An **idiom** is an expression that is widely used but shouldn't be taken literally. An example is, "It's raining cats and dogs." A **proverb** is a short saying that offers advice. An example is, "Two wrongs don't make a right."

Analogies

Name: _____ Date: _____

Directions: Use a word from the Word Bank to complete each analogy.

Word Bank			
abundant	appliance	arrogance	attendance
defiant	endurance	extravagant	ignorant
insurance	observant	pregnancy	vacancy

1. **18 years** is to **childhood** as **9 months** is to _____

2. **"Sure thing!"** is to **compliant** as **"NO!"** is to _____

3. **concert** is to **turnout** as **classroom** is to _____

4. **couch** is to **furniture** as **toaster** is to _____

5. **available job** is to **opening** as **available room** is to _____

6. **$30 shoes** is to **practical** as **$3,000 shoes** is to _____

7. **counselor** is to **wise** as **detective** is to _____

8. **know a lot** is to **knowledgeable** as **know very little** is to _____

9. **water in the desert** is to **scarce** as **water in the jungle** is to _____

10. **sprinters** is to **speed** as **marathon runners** is to _____

11. **humble** is to **humility** as **conceited** is to _____

12. **future spending** is to **savings account** as **disaster protection** is to _____

UNIT 19

–ent and –ence Endings

- affluent
- apparent
- competent
- condolences
- consequence
- consistency
- eloquent
- equivalent
- frequency
- incompetent
- independence
- indifferent
- interference
- permanent
- persistent
- preference
- presidency
- prevalent
- superintendent
- turbulence

Focus

This week's focus is on multisyllabic words that end with –ent, –ence, or –ency. The –ent suffix signifies a noun or adjective. When –ent changes to –ence or –ency, it changes an adjective to a noun.

Helpful Hint

Notice that all the words on this list end with –ent or –ence. The –ent ending is usually used with adjectives (eloquent, persistent). Adjectives that end with –ent become nouns when –ent is changed to –ence (independent/independence, turbulent/turbulence) or –ency (consistent/consistency, frequent/frequency).

🔍 See the Digital Resources for additional spelling activities.

Sentence Completions

Name: _____ **Date:** _____

Directions: Use a word from the Word Bank to complete each sentence.

Word Bank			
affluent	apparent	eloquent	equivalent
frequency	incompetent	indifferent	interference
persistent	presidency	superintendent	turbulence

1. We complained about the boys' _____ when they kept running through our game.

2. My dog is _____ to my new hamster. She acts like the hamster's not even there.

3. After his fifth scheduling mistake, Bryan's boss decided he was _____ and fired him.

4. Let's move the party indoors. It's _____ that the rain isn't going to stop for a while.

5. How many times did Obama travel to Europe during his _____ ?

6. Lena's family is very _____. They own three homes and a private jet.

7. We praised Keisha for giving such an _____ speech during the Earth Day assembly.

8. You should see the doctor about your _____ cough. It's been lingering for three weeks!

9. Are three teaspoons _____ to a tablespoon?

10. The pilot turned the seatbelt sign back on when the plane started to hit

   _____ .

11. The _____ is in charge of all 10 schools in our town. She tells the principals what to do.

12. We increased the _____ of my guitar lessons. Now I go twice a week instead of once.

Name: _____ **Date:** _____

Directions: Use a word from the Word Bank for each section.

Word Bank

affluent	apparent	competent	condolences
consequence	eloquent	equivalent	independence
indifferent	permanent	persistent	prevalent

Write a synonym for each word.

1. freedom _____
2. wealthy _____
3. skilled _____
4. obvious _____

Write an antonym for each word.

5. congratulations _____
6. uncommon _____
7. temporary _____
8. unequal _____

Write a word that fits each category.

9. well-spoken, articulate, smooth, _____

10. determined, stubborn, relentless, _____

11. not interested, unconcerned, apathetic, _____

12. result, outcome, effect, _____

Prefixes, Suffixes, and Roots

Name: _____ **Date:** _____

Directions: Did you know that the root *sist* comes from a Latin word that means *stand* or *hold a place*? Use a word from the Word Bank to match each definition.

Word Bank			
assist	assistance	assistant	consistent
consists	inconsistent	insist	irresistible
persist	persistent	resist	resistance

1. _____ say no to temptation or an enemy; **stand** your ground *(verb)*

2. _____ a refusal to accept or give in; the **standing** of one's ground *(noun)*

3. _____ so tempting that a person is not able to **stand** his ground and say no *(adjective)*

4. _____ **stand** beside a person and help him or her do work *(verb)*

5. _____ a person who **stands** beside someone and helps him or her do work *(noun)*

6. _____ the act of **standing** beside someone and helping with work *(noun)*

7. _____ is made or composed of; **stands** firm because of *(verb)*

8. _____ regular or predictable; **standing** the same way every time *(adjective)*

9. _____ not regular or predictable; not **standing** the same way every time *(adjective)*

10. _____ keep going; stay **standing** in spite of opposition or hurdles *(verb)*

11. _____ stubbornly determined; still **standing** and refusing to give up *(adjective)*

12. _____ demand action or state your mind firmly; take a **stand** *(verb)*

Name: _____ Date:_____

Directions: Read each idiom, phrase, or proverb, and write a sentence explaining its meaning.

1. **Absence** makes the heart grow fonder.

_____

_____

_____

2. **Innocent** until proven guilty.

_____

_____

_____

3. **Silence** is golden.

_____

_____

_____

4. **Different** strokes for different folks.

_____

_____

_____

An **idiom** is an expression that is widely used but shouldn't be taken literally. An example is, "It's raining cats and dogs." A **proverb** is a short saying that offers advice. An example is, "Two wrongs don't make a right."

Analogies

Name: _____ Date: _____

Directions: Use a word from the Word Bank to complete each analogy.

Word Bank			
condolences	consequence	consistency	equivalent
frequency	independence	indifferent	interference
permanent	presidency	superintendent	turbulence

1. **wedding** is to **congratulations** as **funeral** is to _____

2. **how much** is to **quantity** as **how often** is to _____

3. **sweet** is to **flavor** as **thick** is to _____

4. **school** is to **principal** as **district** is to _____

5. **rough boat ride** is to **choppy water** as **rough flight** is to _____

6. **pencil** is to **erasable** as **pen** is to _____

7. $\frac{1}{2}$ and $\frac{1}{4}$ is to **unequal** as $\frac{1}{2}$ and $\frac{2}{4}$ is to _____

8. **Veterans Day** is to **military sacrifices** as **4th of July** is to _____

9. **intervene** is to **intervention** as **interfere** is to _____

10. **lying** is to **bad behavior** as **no screens for a week** is to _____

11. **"I can't wait!"** is to **excited** as **"I don't care."** is to _____

12. **Office of the Governor** is to **governorship** as **Office of the President** is to

    _____

UNIT 20
–ate Ending

Focus

This week's focus is on multisyllabic words that end with *–ate*. The last syllable of each word has a short *i* sound.

Helpful Hint

Notice that all the words on this list end with *–ate*. They are nouns (*vertebrate*) or adjectives (*unfortunate*), and the *–ate* ending is pronounced with a short *i* sound. Many of the words can also be used as verbs, in which case the pronunciation changes. The *–ate* ending takes on a long *a* sound (*associate*, *duplicate*, *moderate*).

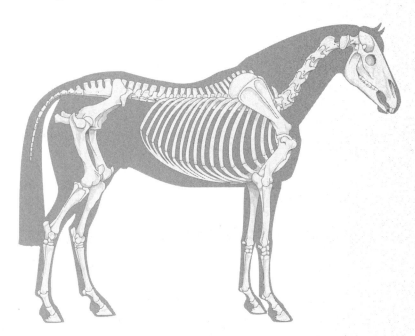

- adequate
- advocate
- affectionate
- approximate
- articulate
- associate
- compassionate
- coordinate
- desolate
- duplicate
- illiterate
- immaculate
- inanimate
- inappropriate
- intermediate
- intricate
- legitimate
- moderate
- unfortunate
- vertebrate

See the Digital Resources for additional spelling activities.

Name: _____ **Date:** _____

Directions: Use a word from the Word Bank to complete each sentence.

Word Bank			
advocate	approximate	coordinate	desolate
illiterate	immaculate	inanimate	inappropriate
intricate	legitimate	moderate	unfortunate

1. Rocks are _____ objects because they don't eat, breathe, grow, or reproduce.

2. It's _____ that Logan missed his flight and won't be here in time for the ceremony.

3. The children's party clothes were _____ until they started playing in the dirt.

4. Mrs. Gupta doesn't take off points if we have a _____ reason for handing our work in late.

5. We had a _____ amount of rain last spring, but not enough to cause flooding.

6. Just give me an _____ number of guests so I know how much food to buy.

7. We learned how to plot points during our _____ graphing unit in math.

8. The fairground looked so _____ after the fair ended. It was just a dusty, empty lot.

9. Mason has been an _____ for shelter pets since he was six. He even started a charity to help them.

10. It would be _____ to wear pajamas to a job interview.

11. Many of the settlers were _____ because they never had the opportunity to go to school.

12. Janessa's comforter has an _____ floral design on one side and bold stripes on the other.

Name: _____ **Date:** _____

Directions: Use a word from the Word Bank for each section.

Word Bank			
adequate	advocate	affectionate	articulate
associate	desolate	immaculate	inanimate
intricate	legitimate	moderate	unfortunate

Write a synonym for each word.

1. loving _____
2. enough _____
3. spotless _____
4. eloquent _____

Write an antonym for each word.

5. lucky _____
6. alive _____
7. simple _____

Write a word that fits each category.

8. genuine, authentic, valid, _____
9. supporter, promoter, champion, _____
10. average, medium, in the middle, _____
11. empty, deserted, bleak, _____
12. partner, colleague, coworker, _____

Name: _____ **Date:** _____

Directions: Did you know that the roots *ply* and *plic* come from a Latin word that means *fold, lay,* or *bend*? Use a word from the Word Bank to match each definition.

Word Bank			
application	apply	complicate	complicated
duplicate	explicit	implicit	imply
multiply	pliable	replicate	reply

1. _____ respond; **bend** back to the speaker with an answer (*verb*)

2. _____ add more **layers** to a challenge; make a problem more difficult (*verb*)

3. _____ **layered** with difficulty (*adjective*)

4. _____ spread a **layer** of sunscreen or paint on a surface (*verb*)

5. _____ a coating or **layer** of paint or sunscreen (*noun*)

6. _____ a copy of a house key or document; an object that is identical to the original, such as two **folded** halves of a paper (*noun*)

7. _____ repeat an action or result; **fold** something over and over again (*verb*)

8. _____ get bigger; increase two**fold**, three**fold**, etc. (*verb*)

9. _____ hint at; **fold** a deeper meaning into your words (*verb*)

10. _____ able to **fold** or **bend** easily (*adjective*)

11. _____ fully expressed and obvious; "**unfolded**" (*adjective*)

12. _____ not having an obvious meaning; partially hidden or "**folded up**" (*adjective*)

Name: _____ **Date:** _____

Directions: Your principal needs a new sixth grade teacher and has asked you to be part of the hiring committee. Your first task is to write a paragraph that describes the type of teacher you're looking for. What skills, qualities, and knowledge will the teacher need? What types of tasks will he or she perform during the school day? Use a minimum of six sentences and six –*ate* words.

Word Bank				
accurate	appropriate	calculate	captivate	celebrate
chocolate	communicate	compassionate	coordinate	create
decorate	demonstrate	educate	elaborate	fascinate
illustrate	immediate	motivate	navigate	ultimate

_____

_____

_____

_____

_____

_____

_____

_____

_____

_____

_____

_____

_____

_____

_____

_____

_____

Here's the Scenario

Analogies

Name: _____ Date: _____

Directions: Use a word from the Word Bank to complete each analogy.

Word Bank			
associate	coordinates	desolate	duplicate
illiterate	immaculate	inanimate	intermediate
intricate	moderate	unfortunate	vertebrate

1. **snail** is to **invertebrate** as **monkey** is to _____

2. **lizard** is to **animate** as **pebble** is to _____

3. **playroom** is to **messy** as **operating room** is to _____

4. **teacher** is to **colleague** as **businessman** is to _____

5. **extra tire** is to **spare** as **extra key** is to _____

6. **can't be read** is to **illegible** as **can't read** is to _____

7. **second grade** is to **primary** as **fourth grade** is to _____

8. **misplace $1,000** is to **disastrous** as **misplace $10** is to _____

9. **10-piece puzzle** is to **simple** as **1,000-piece puzzle** is to _____

10. **bottom of a graph** is to *x*-axis as **points on a graph** is to _____

11. **school playground** is to **bustling** as **abandoned lot** is to _____

12. **very high or very low** is to **extreme** as **in the middle** is to _____

UNIT 21

-ity Ending

Focus

This week's focus is on multisyllabic words that end with –*ity*. The derivational suffix –*ity* changes an adjective to a noun.

Helpful Hint

Notice that all the words on this list are nouns that end with –*ity*. The –*ity* suffix can change an adjective to a noun. For example, *national* becomes *nationality* and *secure* becomes *security*. When an adjective ends with –*le*, the noun form is created by replacing –*le* with –*ility* (*possible/possibility*, *responsible/responsibility*, *stable/stability*).

➤ authority
➤ capacity
➤ curiosity
➤ electricity
➤ equality
➤ facility
➤ fidelity
➤ hospitality
➤ hostility
➤ humidity
➤ intensity
➤ nationality
➤ necessity
➤ opportunity
➤ personality
➤ possibility
➤ priority
➤ responsibility
➤ security
➤ university

See the Digital Resources for additional spelling activities.

Name: _____ **Date:** _____

Directions: Use a word from the Word Bank to complete each sentence.

Word Bank			
authority	capacity	electricity	facility
fidelity	humidity	intensity	necessity
opportunity	priority	responsibility	security

1. This _____ is making me sweat more than the temperature!

2. A _____ guard patrolled the area to make sure no one was trespassing.

3. There's no _____ at the campground, so we always cook over a fire.

4. I'm so lucky that my aunt gave me the _____ to travel to Europe with her!

5. My teacher doesn't have the _____ to cancel school on snow days.

6. Scientists use a rating scale to measure the _____ of hurricanes.

7. I can't wait until they build an indoor soccer _____ in our town!

8. Jaidon follows the rules of his religion with _____ .

9. We need a bigger car, one with the _____ to hold at least six people.

10. You don't need a fire extinguisher on your boat, but life jackets are a

    _____ .

11. When I become student council president, my first _____ is to change the lunch menu.

12. Babysitting toddlers is a huge _____ . You can't take your eyes off them for a second!

Name: _____   Date: _____

Directions: Use a word from the Word Bank for each section.

Synonyms and Antonyms

Word Bank			
authority	curiosity	facility	fidelity
hostility	humidity	intensity	nationality
necessity	opportunity	security	university

Write a synonym for each word or phrase.

1. safety _____

2. degree of
   strength or energy _____

3. power _____

4. country of
   origin _____

Write an antonym for each word.

5. luxury _____

6. friendliness _____

7. indifference _____

8. unfaithfulness _____

Write a word that fits each category.

9. temperature, precipitation, wind speed, _____

10. school, college, academy, _____

11. building, structure, establishment, _____

12. lucky chance, big break, option, _____

Name: _____ **Date:** _____

Prefixes, Suffixes, and Roots

Directions: Did you know that the root *fid* comes from a Latin word that means *belief*, *faith*, or *trust*? Use a word from the Word Bank to match each definition.

Word Bank			
affidavit	bona fide	confidant	confide
confidence	confident	confidential	diffidence
diffident	fidelity	Fido	infidel

1. _____ put your **trust** in someone by sharing your secrets or deep thoughts (*verb*)

2. _____ **faithfulness**; loyalty (*noun*)

3. _____ having **faith** or trust in oneself (*adjective*)

4. _____ **faith** or trust in oneself (*noun*)

5. _____ a close friend; someone with whom you **trust** secrets and deep thoughts (*noun*)

6. _____ private or secret; not to be shared or **entrusted** with everyone (*adjective*)

7. _____ shy; lacking **faith** in oneself (*adjective*)

8. _____ shyness; a lack of **faith** in oneself (*noun*)

9. _____ a written statement that is made in good **faith** and is used in a court case (*noun*)

10. _____ a popular name for dogs, who are known to be **loyal** and **faithful** pets (*noun*)

11. _____ a non**believer**; a person who doesn't **believe** in or follow a religion (*noun*)

12. _____ genuine; made or carried out in good **faith** (*adjective*)

Name: _____ **Date:** _____

Directions: Read each idiom or proverb, and write a sentence explaining its meaning.

1. **Variety** is the spice of life.

   _____

   _____

   _____

2. In the middle of difficulty lies **opportunity**.

   _____

   _____

   _____

3. **Curiosity** killed the cat.

   _____

   _____

   _____

4. **Necessity** is the mother of invention.

   _____

   _____

   _____

An **idiom** is an expression that is widely used, but shouldn't be taken literally. An example is, "It's raining cats and dogs." A **proverb** is a short saying that offers advice. An example is, "Two wrongs don't make a right."

Name: _____   Date:_____

Directions: Use a word from the Word Bank to complete each analogy.

Word Bank			
capacity	electricity	equality	hostility
humidity	intensity	nationality	necessity
personality	possibility	responsibility	university

1. **Revolutionary War** is to **freedom** as **Civil Rights Movement** is to _____

2. **Jewish** is to **religion** as **Russian** is to _____

3. **hot** is to **temperature** as **muggy** is to _____

4. **teacher** is to **high school** as **professor** is to _____

5. **pounds** is to **weight** as **gallons** is to _____

6. **pipes** is to **water** as **wires** is to _____

7. **pretty** is to **appearance** as **kind** is to _____

8. **vacation home** is to **luxury** as **home** is to _____

9. **hug** is to **affection** as **shove** is to _____

10. **playing a video game** is to **pastime** as **feeding the dog** is to _____

11. **make louder** is to **volume** as **make stronger** is to _____

12. **definitely** is to **certainty** as **maybe** is to _____

UNIT 22
-ary Ending

Focus

This week's focus is on multisyllabic words that end with *–ary*. The *–ary* ending can be used with nouns or adjectives.

Helpful Hint

Notice that all the words on this list end with *–ary*. Words that end with *–ary* can be nouns (*capillary*, *vocabulary*) or adjectives (*exemplary*, *sanitary*). Occasionally, a noun can be changed into an adjective by adding the *–ary* suffix (*revolution/revolutionary*, *custom/customary*).

➤ anniversary
➤ capillary
➤ commentary
➤ complimentary
➤ culinary
➤ customary
➤ documentary
➤ exemplary
➤ extraordinary
➤ hereditary
➤ imaginary
➤ infirmary
➤ involuntary
➤ itinerary
➤ monetary
➤ obituary
➤ revolutionary
➤ salivary
➤ sanitary
➤ vocabulary

See the Digital Resources for additional spelling activities.

Name: _____ Date: _____

Directions: Use a word from the Word Bank to complete each sentence.

Sentence Completions

Word Bank			
commentary	complimentary	customary	documentary
extraordinary	hereditary	itinerary	monetary
obituary	revolutionary	salivary	sanitary

1. Dad listened to sports _____ on the radio during our entire road trip.

2. My great-grandmother's ring has very little _____ value since the diamond is fake.

3. Doctors test for a range of _____ diseases as soon as a baby is born.

4. According to the _____ , Mr. Garcia's funeral will take place tomorrow at 10:00 a.m.

5. The chef uses _____ practices in the kitchen so her patrons won't get food poisoning.

6. We had an _____ view of the solar eclipse at my uncle's farm last summer.

7. Nate stopped eating chicken after he watched a disturbing _____ about factory farms.

8. Serena and Amal are excited about their trip. The _____ looks great!

9. The restaurant is giving away _____ cups of coffee to firefighters fighting the wildfire in town.

10. In some cultures, it's _____ to greet friends with a bow instead of a handshake.

11. The invention of the smallpox vaccine in 1796 was _____ . For the first time, doctors could stop a disease before a patient even got sick!

12. Humans have three pairs of _____ glands in their mouths to secrete spit, or saliva.

Name: _____ **Date:** _____

Directions: Use a word from the Word Bank for each section.

Word Bank			
capillary	complimentary	culinary	customary
exemplary	hereditary	imaginary	involuntary
itinerary	monetary	sanitary	vocabulary

Write a synonym for each word or phrase.

1. genetic _____

2. financial _____

3. related to
   cooking _____

4. collection
   of words _____

Write an antonym for each word or phrase.

5. real _____

6. on purpose _____

7. mediocre _____

8. unusual _____

Write a word that fits each category.

9. clean, hygienic, germ-free, _____

10. agenda, schedule, list of events, _____

11. free, no charge, on the house, _____

12. artery, vessel, vein, _____

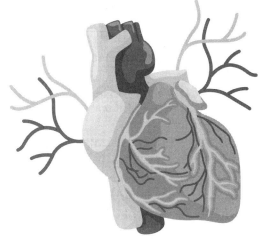

Name: _____ **Date:** _____

Directions: The root *vol* comes from a Latin word that means *wish* or *will*. The root *firm* comes from a Latin word that means *strong* or *steady*. Use a word from the Word Bank to match each definition.

Word Bank			
affirm	affirmation	benevolent	confirm
confirmation	infirmary	involuntary	malevolent
reaffirm	unconfirmed	voluntary	volunteer

1. _____ evil; showing bad **will** (*adjective*)

2. _____ kind; showing good **will** (*adjective*)

3. _____ a person who **willingly** steps up to help (*noun*)

4. _____ not forced; done **willingly** (*adjective*)

5. _____ done without **will** or conscious control (*adjective*)

6. _____ a place where sick or injured people receive care until they're **strong** again (*noun*)

7. _____ make plans or beliefs **stronger** (*verb*)

8. _____ the process of making plans or beliefs **stronger** by providing evidence (*noun*)

9. _____ not proven true or accurate yet; not having **strong** evidence (*adjective*)

10. _____ say yes; express a **strong** belief or dedication to an idea (*verb*)

11. _____ say yes again; state a belief again **strongly** (*verb*)

12. _____ provides **strength** by saying yes to the choices that have been made (*noun*)

Name: _____ Date: _____

Directions: Answer each question in a complete sentence. Remember to turn the question around, and use the bold word in your answer.

1. Why do campers need to visit the **infirmary**?

   _____

   _____

2. What can you learn about a person from their **obituary**?

   _____

   _____

3. Why do you think children should receive **monetary** rewards for doing chores?

   _____

   _____

4. Why do grocery stores give away **complimentary** food samples?

   _____

   _____

5. Why is it important to improve your **vocabulary**?

   _____

   _____

6. Why is it important to use **sanitary** practices in the kitchen?

   _____

   _____

Turn the Question Around

Name: _____ **Date:** _____

Directions: Use a word from the Word Bank to complete each analogy.

Word Bank			
anniversary	capillary	complimentary	culinary
extraordinary	hereditary	imaginary	infirmary
itinerary	obituary	Revolutionary	vocabulary

1. **nonfiction** is to **real** as **fiction** is to _____

2. **hungry** is to **dining hall** as **sick** is to _____

3. **trunk** is to **twig** as **artery** is to _____

4. **author's bio** is to **book jacket** as **deceased person's bio** is to _____

5. **hair length** is to **choice** as **height** is to _____

6. **1860s war** is to **Civil** as **1770s war** is to _____

7. **meeting** is to **agenda** as **vacation** is to _____

8. **years of life** is to **birthday** as **years of marriage** is to _____

9. **sunrise and sunset** is to **ordinary** as **eclipse** is to _____

10. **for a few dollars** is to **cheap** as **for free** is to _____

11. **facts I know** is to **background knowledge** as **words I know** is to _____

12. **mechanics** is to **automotive** as **cooking school** is to _____

UNIT 23

-ory Ending

Focus

This week's focus is on multisyllabic words that end with *–ory*. The *–ory* ending can be used with nouns or adjectives.

Helpful Hint

Notice that all the words on this list end with *–ory*. Words that end with *–ory* can be nouns (*dormitory, laboratory*) or adjectives (*introductory, satisfactory*). The *–ory* suffix is often added to nouns that end with *–or* (*predator/predatory*) or verbs that end with *–ate* (*migrate/migratory, discriminate/discriminatory, obligate/obligatory*).

➤ accessory
➤ accusatory
➤ auditory
➤ circulatory
➤ contradictory
➤ derogatory
➤ discriminatory
➤ dormitory
➤ inflammatory
➤ introductory
➤ laboratory
➤ lavatory
➤ migratory
➤ obligatory
➤ observatory
➤ predatory
➤ respiratory
➤ satisfactory
➤ self-explanatory
➤ trajectory

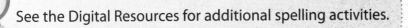

See the Digital Resources for additional spelling activities.

Name: _____ Date: _____

Sentence Completions

Directions: Use a word from the Word Bank to complete each sentence.

Word Bank			
accessory	accusatory	circulatory	contradictory
discriminatory	inflammatory	laboratory	lavatory
obligatory	observatory	self-explanatory	trajectory

1.   The scientists conduct experiments in their _____ .

2.   Doctors determine how well your _____ system is working by measuring blood pressure.

3.   NASA studied the meteor's _____ and determined it would crash into the ocean.

4.   You can read the manual, but all the camera buttons should be

_____ .

5.   Keep your seatbelt buckled unless you need to use the airplane's

_____ .

6.   Rosa Parks fought against _____ policies when she refused to give up her seat on the bus.

7.   The weather reports were _____ . One predicted rain, but the other predicted sunshine.

8.   The speaker's _____ remarks about race caused the crowd to stand up and start booing.

9.   Jackie's favorite _____ is a pink satin scarf that she wears to school at least twice a week.

10.   Why did you use such an _____ tone when you asked where the package of cookies went?

11.   David gave each of his aunts an _____ hug and kiss, and he went to play with his cousins.

12.   The 94th floor _____ in the Hancock Building has breathtaking views of Chicago!

Name: _____ **Date:** _____

Directions: Use a word from the Word Bank for each section.

Synonyms and Antonyms

Word Bank			
accessories	derogatory	discriminatory	dormitory
inflammatory	introductory	lavatory	obligatory
predatory	satisfactory	self-explanatory	trajectory

Write a synonym for each word or phrase.

1. required _____

2. path through
   space _____

3. bathroom _____

4. causing anger _____

Write an antonym for each word.

5. flattering _____

6. confusing _____

7. fair _____

8. unacceptable _____

Write a word that fits each category.

9. bedroom, hotel room, hospital room, _____

10. carnivorous, aggressive, hungry, _____

11. clothing, shoes, makeup, _____

12. first, beginning, initial, _____

Prefixes, Suffixes, and Roots

Name: _____ Date: _____

Directions: Did you know that the root *ject* comes from a Latin word that means *throw*? Use a word from the Word Bank to match each definition.

Word Bank			
conjecture	eject	injection	interject
object	objection	project	projectile
projector	rejection	subject	trajectory

1. _____ medicine that has been "**thrown**" into a person's arm with a needle (*noun*)

2. _____ **throw out** a cassette or disk; **throw** a person out of a vehicle (*verb*)

3. _____ the act of **throwing** back a person or idea you don't agree with (*noun*)

4. _____ interrupt a conversation by **throwing** in a comment or remark (*verb*)

5. _____ a machine that **throws** a movie onto a screen (*noun*)

6. _____ **throw** or cast forward, such as a loud voice or a movie on a screen (*verb*)

7. _____ **throw** out your disapproval of a statement or idea, such as in a courtroom (*verb*)

8. _____ an expression of disapproval; an argument that has been **thrown** out (*noun*)

9. _____ the path an object follows when it is **thrown** into the air or space (*noun*)

10. _____ **throw** a person into a dangerous or unpleasant situation (*verb*)

11. _____ an object or missile that is **thrown** into the air with great force (*noun*)

12. _____ an opinion; ideas that have been **thrown** together without all the facts (*noun*)

Name: _____ **Date:** _____

Directions: Write 10 of the words from the Word Bank two times each in your best cursive.

Word Bank				
accessory	accusatory	auditory	circulatory	contradictory
derogatory	discriminatory	dormitory	inflammatory	introductory
laboratory	lavatory	migratory	obligatory	observatory
predatory	respiratory	satisfactory	self-explanatory	trajectory

_____ _____

_____ _____

_____ _____

_____ _____

_____ _____

_____ _____

_____ _____

_____ _____

_____ _____

_____ _____

Name: _____ **Date:** _____

Directions: Use a word from the Word Bank to complete each analogy.

Word Bank			
accessory	accusatory	auditory	derogatory
dormitory	introductory	laboratory	lavatory
migratory	respiratory	satisfactory	self-explanatory

1. **doctor** is to **hospital** as **scientist** is to _____

2. **living room** is to **parlor** as **bathroom** is to _____

3. **heart** is to **circulatory** as **lungs** is to _____

4. **eating** is to **dining hall** as **sleeping** is to _____

5. **vision** is to **optic** as **hearing** is to _____

6. **last lesson** is to **concluding** as **first lesson** is to _____

7. **A+** is to **exemplary** as **B** is to _____

8. **compliment** is to **flattering** as **insult** is to _____

9. **shirt** is to **clothing** as **bracelet** is to _____

10. **"I would never…"** is to **indignant** as **"How dare you…"** is to _____

11. **birds that eat prey** is to **predatory** as **birds that fly south** is to _____

12. **need assistance** is to **complicated** as **don't need assistance** is to

_____

UNIT 24
-ous Ending

- adventurous
- autonomous
- carnivorous
- disastrous
- frivolous
- herbivorous
- indigenous
- ludicrous
- meticulous
- miraculous
- mischievous
- mountainous
- ominous
- omnivorous
- perilous
- prosperous
- ridiculous
- synonymous
- unanimous
- villainous

Focus

This week's focus is on multisyllabic words that end with –ous. The derivational suffix –ous changes a noun to an adjective.

Helpful Hint

Notice that all the words on this list are adjectives that end with –ous. The –ous suffix changes a noun to an adjective (*adventure/ adventurous, omnivore/omnivorous, peril/perilous*) and means "full of."

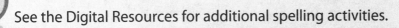

See the Digital Resources for additional spelling activities.

Sentence Completions

Name: _____ **Date:**_____

Directions: Use a word from the Word Bank to complete each sentence.

Word Bank			
adventurous	autonomous	frivolous	indigenous
ludicrous	meticulous	miraculous	ominous
omnivorous	perilous	prosperous	unanimous

1. Instead of spending your money on _____ things, such as candy, you should save it for something important.

2. Horses are not _____ to America. They were brought here by Spanish explorers.

3. When the sky darkened and looked _____ , we packed up and headed home from the beach.

4. None of the doctors expected Lila to survive, but she made a _____ recovery.

5. My neighbor takes _____ care of her lawn. Not a single blade of grass is out of place!

6. Mom thinks the cartoon about the ninja hamburger is _____ , but I think it's funny.

7. Raccoons are obviously _____ because they'll eat anything they find in my garbage cans.

8. Our farm was very _____ last year thanks to new equipment and an ideal growing season.

9. The United States broke away from England in 1776 to become an _____ country.

10. The vote is _____ . We all want to go out for ice cream!

11. My brother is more _____ than I am. He likes to explore the jetty while I lay on the beach.

12. During his _____ journey to the North Pole, Frederick Cook faced terrible weather and drifting ice.

Name: _____ **Date:** _____

Directions: Use a word from the Word Bank for each section.

Word Bank			
autonomous	frivolous	indigenous	ludicrous
meticulous	miraculous	mountainous	ominous
perilous	prosperous	unanimous	villainous

Write a synonym for each word or phrase.

1. native _____

2. threatening _____

3. all in
   agreement _____

4. ridiculous _____

Write an antonym for each word.

5. poor _____

6. heroic _____

7. safe _____

8. important _____

Write a word that fits each category.

9. attentive to detail, careful, conscientious, _____

10. rocky, rugged, steep, _____

11. independent, in control, self-governing, _____

12. amazing, unbelievable, magical, _____

Name: _____ Date:_____

Directions: Did you know that the prefix *auto–* comes from a Greek word that means *self*? Use a word from the Word Bank to match each definition.

Word Bank			
autobiographical	autobiography	autograph	autoimmune
automated	automatic	automobile	automotive
autonomous	autonomy	autopilot	autopsy

1. _____ a book a person writes about her**self** (*noun*)

2. _____ describing a book, movie, or play that a person wrote about him**self** (*adjective*)

3. _____ a vehicle that moves by it**self** without the help of horses or mules (*noun*)

4. _____ relating to motor vehicles, or vehicles that move by them**selves** (*adjective*)

5. _____ done without thinking or without human help; done all by it**self** (*adjective*)

6. _____ a famous person's signature; something she writes her**self** (*noun*)

7. _____ independence; the ability to control and make decisions for one**self** (*noun*)

8. _____ acting independently; having the ability to make decisions for one**self** (*adjective*)

9. _____ a device that allows a vehicle to steer it**self** (*noun*)

10. _____ describing a disease in which the body attacks it**self** (*adjective*)

11. _____ the examination of a body after death; a chance for the examiner to "see for him**self**" what happened (*noun*)

12. _____ describing a machine that controls it**self** without the help of a worker, such as an ATM (*adjective*)

Prefixes, Suffixes, and Roots

Name: _____ Date:_____

Directions: Answer each question in a complete sentence. Remember to turn the question around, and use the bold word in your answer.

1. What are some plants or animals that are **indigenous** to your state?

    _____

    _____

2. Why is it **frivolous** to spend all your money on candy and toys?

    _____

    _____

3. What happens when the sky turns an **ominous** shade of gray?

    _____

    _____

4. Why are hikes up Mount Everest so **perilous**?

    _____

    _____

5. Why are retailers so **prosperous** during the months of November and December?

    _____

    _____

6. Why do pharmacists need to be **meticulous** when they fill prescriptions?

    _____

    _____

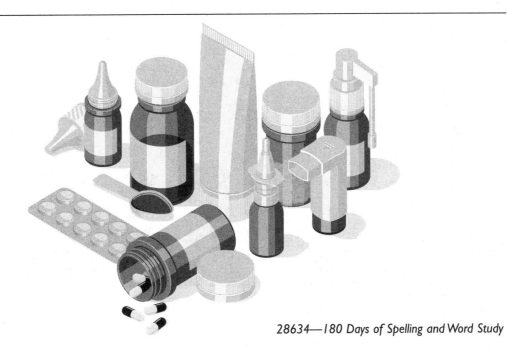

Analogies

Name: _____ Date: _____

Directions: Use a word from the Word Bank to complete each analogy.

Word Bank			
adventurous	carnivorous	disastrous	frivolous
herbivorous	indigenous	mischievous	mountainous
ridiculous	synonymous	unanimous	villainous

1. **bear** is to **omnivorous** as **lion** is to _____

2. **Kansas** is to **flat** as **Colorado** is to _____

3. **no one agrees** is to **divided** as **everyone agrees** is to _____

4. **boots in a snowstorm** is to **sensible** as **sandals in a snowstorm** is to _____

5. **homebody** is to **unadventurous** as **world traveler** is to _____

6. **Red Riding Hood** is to **heroic** as **Big Bad Wolf** is to _____

7. **save money** is to **responsible** as **waste money** is to _____

8. **weekend blizzard** is to **inconvenient** as **rush hour blizzard** is to _____

9. **cactus in Connecticut** is to **non-native** as **cactus in Arizona** is to _____

10. **shark** is to **carnivorous** as **deer** is to _____

11. **happy and sad** is to **dissimilar** as **happy and glad** is to _____

12. **well-behaved child** is to **obedient** as **naughty child** is to _____

28634—180 Days of Spelling and Word Study   © *Shell Education*

UNIT 25
Hard and Soft G Words

- analogy
- apology
- archaeology
- biology
- chronology
- disadvantage
- ecology
- epilogue
- geologist
- geology
- intriguing
- meteorology
- monologue
- mythology
- psychologist
- psychology
- synagogue
- technology
- terminology
- zoology

Focus

This week's focus is on hard and soft sounds of *g* in multisyllabic words. The *–ology* ending is introduced.

Helpful Hint

Notice that all the words on this list have a hard or soft *g* sound in the final syllable. The *–y* at the end of words such as *mythology* and *biology* keeps the *g* soft, since soft *g* is always followed by *e*, *i*, or *y*. It is unusual for multisyllabic words to end with a hard *g* sound, but when they do, they use the *gue* pattern. The *u* acts as a buffer between the *g* and *e* to keep the *g* sound hard (*in·trigue*, *syn·a·gogue*).

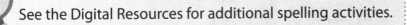

See the Digital Resources for additional spelling activities.

Name: _____ Date:_____

Directions: Use a word from the Word Bank to complete each sentence.

Word Bank			
apology	archaeology	disadvantage	ecology
epilogue	geologist	intriguing	monologue
mythology	psychologist	technology	terminology

1. We learned about the hero's journey during our _____ unit in language arts.

2. I refused to accept Peyton's _____ because she didn't sound sincere.

3. New _____ makes it easier for children with diabetes to monitor their blood sugar.

4. Wangari Maathai was so _____ , I decided to read three biographies about her.

5. Children who've never played an instrument will be at a _____ if they join the eighth-grade band.

6. We had a _____ come to our classroom to teach us about rocks.

7. After my cousin died unexpectedly, a _____ helped me sort out my feelings.

8. I had to write an _____ to my story. It takes place five years after the original ending.

9. I had to memorize a _____ for my role in the school play.

10. It is difficult to explain the problem to the mechanic because I don't know the correct _____ for all the car parts.

11. My favorite part of studying _____ is drawing food chains and food webs.

12. Cristina took an _____ class so she could learn more about ancient civilizations.

Name: _____ **Date:** _____

Directions: Use a word from the Word Bank for each section.

Word Bank			
apology	chronology	disadvantage	epilogue
geologist	intriguing	meteorology	mythology
synagogue	technology	terminology	zoology

Write a synonym for each word or phrase.

1. animal science _____

2. weather science _____

3. rock and mineral scientist _____

4. expression of regret _____

Write an antonym for each word or phrase.

5. boring _____

6. benefit _____

7. prologue _____

8. random order of events _____

Write a word that fits each category.

9. folktales, fairy tales, fables, _____

10. language, word choice, vocabulary, _____

11. mosque, temple, church, _____

12. scientific advances, new inventions, progress, _____

Name: _____ **Date:** _____

Directions: Did you know that the suffix *–logy* comes from Greek and means *word*? At the end of a word, *–logy* usually means *the science or study of something*. Sometimes it means *collection*. Use a word from the Word Bank to match each definition.

Word Bank			
analogy	apology	archaeology	biology
chronology	ecology	geology	meteorology
mythology	psychology	technology	zoology

1. _____ the **study of** animals (*noun*)

2. _____ the **study of** rocks and minerals (*noun*)

3. _____ the **study of** the human mind (*noun*)

4. _____ the **study of** how plants and animals interact in their environment (*noun*)

5. _____ the **study of** weather (not meteors!) (*noun*)

6. _____ the **study of** living things: plants, animals, and humans (*noun*)

7. _____ the **study of** human history, discovered by digging up sites (*noun*)

8. _____ the **study of** problems and their solutions, achieved by creating new tools or knowledge (*noun*)

9. _____ the **study of** events and the order in which they happened (*noun*)

10. _____ the **study of** myths, or traditional tales (*noun*)

11. _____ a relationship between two pairs of **words** (*noun*)

12. _____ **words** that express remorse (*noun*)

Name: _____ **Date:** _____

Directions: Answer each question in a complete sentence. Remember to turn the question around, and use the bold word in your answer.

1. Why are stories usually told in **chronological** order?

    _____

    _____

2. What is one type of **technology** you just can't live without? Why?

    _____

    _____

3. What are three topics a **meteorologist** might discuss on TV?

    _____

    _____

4. Why do students enjoy studying **mythology**?

    _____

    _____

5. Why do **archaeologists** spend so much time digging?

    _____

    _____

6. What are some **disadvantages** of having a summer birthday?

    _____

    _____

Name: _____   Date:_____

Directions: Use a word from the Word Bank to complete each analogy.

Word Bank			
apology	archaeology	biology	disadvantage
epilogue	intriguing	meteorology	monologue
mythology	psychologist	synagogue	technology

1. **Christian** is to **church** as **Jewish** is to _____

2. **"Please."** is to **request** as **"I'm sorry."** is to _____

3. **telescope** is to **astronomy** as **microscope** is to _____

4. **Cinderella** is to **fairy tale** as **Zeus** is to _____

5. **beginning of book** is to **prologue** as **end of book** is to _____

6. **two or more speakers** is to **dialogue** as **one speaker** is to _____

7. **the heart** is to **cardiologist** as **the mind** is to _____

8. **study of animals** is to **zoology** as **study of weather** is to _____

9. **worst subject** is to **boring** as **favorite subject** is to _____

10. **focus on the past** is to **archaeology** as **focus on the future** is to _____

11. **height in basketball** is to **advantage** as **height in horse racing** is to _____

12. **telescopes** is to **astronomy** as **shovels and brushes** is to _____

UNIT 26
eri Pattern

Focus

This week's focus is on multisyllabic words that contain the *eri* pattern.

Helpful Hint

Notice that all the words on this list contain the *eri* pattern. In most words, the *i* makes a long *e* sound (*in·ter·i·or*, *per·i·od*, *·ser·i·al*). In a few words, the *i* makes a short *i* sound (*cler·i·cal*, *ex·per·i·ment*, *se·ver·i·ty*).

🔍 See the Digital Resources for additional spelling activities.

➤ anterior
➤ bacteria
➤ cafeteria
➤ clerical
➤ criteria
➤ deteriorate
➤ experience
➤ experiment
➤ exterior
➤ imperial
➤ inferior
➤ interior
➤ material
➤ mysterious
➤ period
➤ posterior
➤ serial
➤ severity
➤ superior
➤ ulterior

Sentence Completions

Name: _____ Date: _____

Directions: Use a word from the Word Bank to complete each sentence.

Word Bank			
bacteria	clerical	criteria	deteriorate
experiment	inferior	interior	material
posterior	serial	severity	ulterior

1. We're going to _____ with liquids, gases, and solids in science class tomorrow.

2. I suspect Josiah had an _____ motive when he offered to help Mom with the groceries.

3. We won't know the _____ of the flooding until after the rain stops.

4. Some people think American cars are _____ to cars built in Japan, but I prefer them.

5. There are two ligaments in your knee. The _____ ligament crosses behind the anterior one.

6. Mia's vision may _____ if she doesn't get treatment from a doctor soon.

7. I illustrated the _____ of the class book we wrote after Hector illustrated the exterior cover.

8. Every computer, tablet, and cell phone has a unique _____ number printed on it.

9. Read over the _____ for the science fair one more time before you submit your project.

10. Be sure to wash your hands before you cook so you don't get _____ on the food.

11. Mom hired an assistant to help with _____ tasks such as filing, data entry, and scheduling.

12. Steven needs new _____ for his comedy routine. His current jokes aren't funny anymore.

Name: _____ **Date:** _____

Directions: Use a word from the Word Bank for each section.

Synonyms and Antonyms

Word Bank

bacteria	cafeteria	deteriorate	exterior
inferior	material	mysterious	period
posterior	severity	superior	ulterior

Write a synonym for each word.

1. harshness _____
2. fabric _____
3. worsen _____
4. puzzling _____

Write an antonym for each word.

5. modest _____
6. inexperience _____
7. interior _____
8. anterior _____

Write a word that fits each category.

9. comma, exclamation point, quotation marks, _____

10. kitchen, dining hall, dining room, _____

11. germs, microbes, pathogens, _____

12. hidden, underlying, concealed, _____

Name: _____ **Date:** _____

Directions: Did you know that the *–ior* suffix comes from Latin and is used to compare things? Use a word from the Word Bank to match each definition.

Word Bank			
anterior	deteriorate	exterior	inferior
inferiority	interior	posterior	senior
seniority	superior	superiority	ulterior

1. _____ on the outside (*adjective*)

2. _____ on the inside (*adjective*)

3. _____ closer to the front; before (*adjective*)

4. _____ closer to the back; behind (*adjective*)

5. _____ hidden or secret; beyond what is out in the open (*adjective*)

6. _____ of a higher rank, quality, or importance (*adjective*)

7. _____ an attitude of self-importance (*noun*)

8. _____ of a lower rank, quality, or importance (*adjective*)

9. _____ an attitude of decreased self-importance or self-worth (*noun*)

10. _____ older; higher in standard or rank; in twelfth grade (*adjective*)

11. _____ privileged status, earned because someone is older or has more years of service (*noun*)

12. _____ weaken; become worse (*verb*)

Name: _____ **Date:** _____

Directions: Write 10 of the words from the Word Bank two times each in your best cursive.

Word Bank

anterior	bacteria	cafeteria	clerical	criteria
deteriorate	experience	experiment	exterior	imperial
inferior	interior	material	mysterious	period
posterior	serial	severity	superior	ulterior

Name: _____ **Date:** _____

Directions: Use a word from the Word Bank to complete each analogy.

Word Bank			
anterior	bacteria	cafeteria	clerical
criteria	experiment	exterior	imperial
interior	material	period	superior

1. **exclamation** is to **exclamation point** as **statement** is to _____

2. **sculptor** is to **clay** as **dressmaker** is to _____

3. **math** is to **problem** as **science** is to _____

4. **less than** is to **inferior** as **better than** is to _____

5. **country** is to **national** as **empire** is to _____

6. **curtains** is to **interior** as **shutters** is to _____

7. **hotel** is to **dining room** as **school** is to _____

8. **flu** is to **virus** as **strep throat** is to _____

9. **hotel** is to **hospitality** as **office** is to _____

10. **mow** is to **exterior** as **vacuum** is to _____

11. **interior** is to **exterior** as **posterior** is to _____

12. **résumé** is to **qualifications** as **checklist** is to _____

UNIT 27

More *I* Patterns that Sound Like *E*

Focus

This week's focus is on multisyllabic words that contain a long *e* sound. The long *e* sound is represented by the letter *i*.

Helpful Hint

Notice that all the words on this list have a long *e* syllable that is spelled with an *i* (*au·di·ence, id·i·om, ra·di·us*).

See the Digital Resources for additional spelling activities.

- alleviate
- audience
- colonial
- custodian
- disobedient
- equilibrium
- gymnasium
- humiliate
- idiom
- idiosyncrasy
- marsupial
- memorial
- menial
- nutrients
- podium
- portfolio
- radiant
- radius
- recipient
- trivial

Name: _____ **Date:** _____

Directions: Use a word from the Word Bank to complete each sentence.

Word Bank			
alleviate	colonial	equilibrium	humiliate
idiom	idiosyncrasies	marsupial	memorial
menial	portfolio	radiant	recipient

1. My brother tried to _____ me by showing everyone photos of my terrible haircut.

2. Did you know that the opossum is the only _____ native to North America?

3. Assembling an art _____ is a great way to showcase your best work to art schools.

4. The bride looked absolutely _____ when she walked down the aisle.

5. Rubbing aloe on your skin will _____ some of the discomfort of sunburn.

6. Each scholarship _____ was presented an award at the end of the year ceremony.

7. Sam helped his elderly neighbor with _____ tasks, such as washing dishes and leaf blowing.

8. Spinning in circles will throw off your _____ and make you feel dizzy!

9. After Grampy's death, our friends and family paid their respects at a

    _____ service.

10. Atasi doesn't let any of the foods on her plate touch. That's just one of her

    _____ .

11. During my favorite social studies unit, we learned about _____ America.

12. Do people really get butterflies in their stomach or is that just an

    _____ ?

Name: _____ **Date:** _____

Directions: Use a word from the Word Bank for each section.

Word Bank			
alleviate	audience	custodian	equilibrium
humiliate	idiom	memorial	menial
radiant	radius	recipient	trivial

Write a synonym for each word or phrase.

1. glowing with happiness _____

2. embarrass _____

3. lessen pain _____

4. expression or saying _____

Write an antonym for each word or phrase.

5. performer _____

6. lack of balance _____

7. important _____

8. skilled _____

Write a word that fits each category.

9. janitor, housekeeper, maid, _____

10. diameter, circumference, arc, _____

11. tribute, remembrance, monument, _____

12. receiver, beneficiary, heir, _____

Prefixes, Suffixes, and Roots

Name: _____ Date: _____

Directions: Did you know that *rad* comes from a Latin word that means *ray* or *spoke of a wheel*? The root *equ* comes from a Latin word that means *equal*. Use a word from the Word Bank to match each definition.

Word Bank			
adequate	equation	equator	equilibrium
equitable	inadequate	radiant	radiate
radiation	radio	radiology	radius

1. _____   shoot out **rays** of light in every direction (*verb*)

2. _____   energy that comes from waves or **rays**; small amounts are used for x-**rays** (*noun*)

3. _____   a device that is used to transmit or receive sound **waves** across a distance (*noun*)

4. _____   glowing; shooting **rays** of love, confidence, or happiness (*adjective*)

5. _____   a line segment that extends from the middle of a circle to the edge, such as a wheel's **spoke** (*noun*)

6. _____   the study of x-**rays** used for the diagnosis and treatment of disease (*noun*)

7. _____   **equal** balance; the ability to stand upright without getting dizzy (*noun*)

8. _____   fair; divided up **equally** (*adjective*)

9. _____   fair enough; **equal** to a person's demands or expectations (*adjective*)

10. _____   not fair enough; not **equal** to a person's demands or expectations (*adjective*)

11. _____   an imaginary line that divides the Earth into two **equal** hemispheres (*noun*)

12. _____   a number sentence that uses an **equal** sign to show the same value (*noun*)

Name: _____   **Date:** _____

Directions: Answer each question in a complete sentence. Remember to turn the question around, and use the bold word in your answer.

1. Why do brides and grooms look **radiant** on their wedding day?

    _____

    _____

2. What are some strategies students can use to **alleviate** stress before a big test?

    _____

    _____

3. Why might someone be called up to a **podium**?

    _____

    _____

4. What is a roadside **memorial**?

    _____

    _____

5. Why should children help their parents with **menial** tasks?

    _____

    _____

6. Why do people learning English have a hard time understanding **idioms**?

    _____

    _____

Name: _____   **Date:** _____

Directions: Use a word from the Word Bank to complete each analogy.

Word Bank

alleviate	audience	custodian	gymnasium
idiom	marsupial	nutrients	podium
portfolio	radius	recipient	trivial

1. **as big as a house** is to **simile** as **raining cats and dogs** is to _____

2. **hotel room** is to **maid** as **classroom** is to _____

3. **performs** is to **actor** as **claps** is to _____

4. **courses and grades** is to **transcript** as **work samples** is to _____

5. **inheritance** is to **heir** as **scholarship** is to _____

6. **world news** is to **important** as **gossip** is to _____

7. **preacher** is to **pulpit** as **politician** is to _____

8. **whole circle** is to **diameter** as **half circle** is to _____

9. **monkey** is to **primate** as **kangaroo** is to _____

10. **candy** is to **empty calories** as **fruits and vegetables** is to _____

11. **football** is to **field** as **basketball** is to _____

12. **antibiotics** is to **heal** as **pain relievers** is to _____

28634—180 Days of Spelling and Word Study

UNIT 28
ci Words

Focus

This week's focus is on multisyllabic words that have *ci* before the suffix. When *ci* appears before a vowel suffix such as *–er, –ent,* or *–al,* it takes on a /sh/ or /ch/ sound.

Helpful Hint

Notice that all the words on this list have *ci* before the suffix. When *ci* appears before a suffix such as *–ous, –able,* or *–ent,* it makes a /sh/ sound (*a·tro·cious, so·cia·ble, in·suf·fi·cient*). If *n* precedes *ci* or *sci,* it makes a /ch/ sound instead (*un·con·scious*). The *–ian* suffix is used to name a type of person. When *–ian* is added to a word that ends with *c,* the hard *c* becomes soft (*electric/electrician, politic/politician, technic/technician*).

- appreciation
- association
- atrocious
- beneficial
- depreciate
- electrician
- insufficient
- judicious
- magician
- malicious
- mathematician
- musician
- pediatrician
- physician
- politician
- sociable
- specialty
- suspicious
- technician
- unconscious

See the Digital Resources for additional spelling activities.

Sentence Completions

Name: _____ Date: _____

Directions: Use a word from the Word Bank to complete each sentence.

Word Bank			
association	atrocious	beneficial	depreciate
insufficient	judicious	malicious	pediatrician
sociable	specialty	suspicious	unconscious

1. Pies are Jermaine's _____ , but he also bakes delicious cakes and cookies.

2. Our condo _____ is having a meeting next week to discuss new parking rules.

3. Be _____ with your spending, or you'll run out of money before payday.

4. A foul ball flew into the stands, hit Alexis in the head, and knocked her

    _____ .

5. An extra hour of sleep each night would be _____ to your health.

6. I can't understand why Charlotte would spread such _____ lies about me!

7. We heard a _____ noise outside, so we climbed out of bed and peeked out the window.

8. The value of this house will never _____ because everyone wants to live near the beach.

9. Max's table manners are _____ . Watching him eat makes me gag!

10. Sofia had to put some groceries back because she had _____ funds in her account.

11. My _____ did a strep test and then gave me a prescription for antibiotics.

12. Most children are _____ at lunch, but some just want to eat their meal quietly.

Name: _____ **Date:** _____

Directions: Use a word from the Word Bank for each section.

Word Bank

appreciation	association	atrocious	beneficial
depreciate	electrician	insufficient	judicious
malicious	pediatrician	sociable	suspicious

Write a synonym for each word or phrase.

1. wise _____

2. horrible _____

3. lose value _____

4. good for you _____

Write an antonym for each word or phrase.

5. ungratefulness _____

6. kind _____

7. shy _____

8. more than enough _____

Write a word that fits each category.

9. group, organization, council, _____

10. surgeon, allergist, dermatologist, _____

11. distrustful, skeptical, wary, _____

12. builder, plumber, roofer, _____

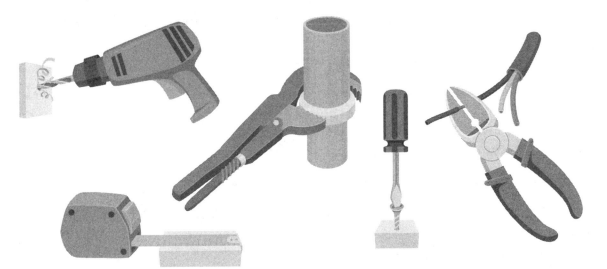

Name: _____   Date: _____

Directions: Did you know that the suffix *–ian* names a type of person? Change each word to a type of person by adding the suffix *–ian*. Notice how the pronunciation of the final *c* changes when you add a suffix.

1. politic   _____
2. mathematic   _____
3. pediatric   _____
4. electric   _____
5. statistic   _____

6. technic   _____
7. magic   _____
8. music   _____
9. physic   _____
10. optic   _____

Directions: Choose a word from your answers to complete each sentence.

11. My little brother cries when he sees the _____ because he's worried about getting a shot.

12. Dad hired a _____ to perform tricks at my sister's birthday party.

13. Jada is an amazing _____ . She's only six, but can already multiply three-digit numbers!

14. Does a _____ spend most of her time campaigning and giving speeches?

15. We hired an _____ to install new lighting in our kitchen.

16. You should always consult your _____ before taking any new medications or vitamins.

17. A computer _____ came to the house to fix our internet problems.

18. Sully is a _____ . He writes his own songs and plays them on the piano.

Name: _____ **Date:** _____

Directions: Answer each question in a complete sentence. Remember to turn the question around, and use the bold word in your answer.

1. What happens when a person writes a check, but there are **insufficient** funds in his or her bank account?

   _____

   _____

2. Why does the value of a car **depreciate** over time?

   _____

   _____

3. Why should people be **judicious** when they invest their money?

   _____

   _____

4. Do asleep and **unconscious** mean the same thing? Explain.

   _____

   _____

5. How can you show **appreciation** to your parents?

   _____

   _____

6. What are **malicious** rumors?

   _____

   _____

Turn the Question Around

Analogies

Name: _____ Date: _____

Directions: Use a word from the Word Bank to complete each analogy.

Word Bank			
appreciation	beneficial	depreciate	electrician
magician	malicious	mathematician	musician
pediatrician	physician	politician	unconscious

1. **animals** is to **veterinarian** as **children** is to _____

2. **funny wig** is to **clown** as **top hat** is to _____

3. **pipes** is to **plumber** as **wiring** is to _____

4. **sympathy card** is to **condolences** as **thank you card** is to _____

5. **paint** is to **artist** as **instrument** is to _____

6. **in bed** is to **asleep** as **on a stretcher** is to _____

7. **hire** is to **employee** as **elect** is to _____

8. **law school** is to **lawyer** as **medical school** is to _____

9. **science** is to **scientist** as **math** is to _____

10. **rain during a flood** is to **damaging** as **rain during a drought** is to _____

11. **praise** is to **kind** as **gossip** is to _____

12. **increase value** is to **appreciate** as **lose value** is to _____

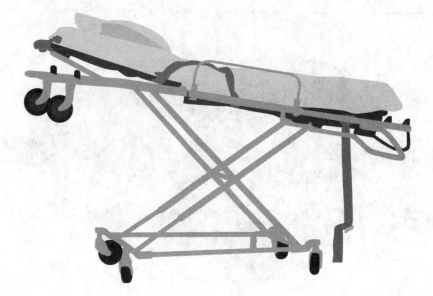

UNIT 29
–eous and –ious Endings

- ambitious
- anxious
- cautious
- conscientious
- contagious
- courageous
- gorgeous
- hilarious
- igneous
- industrious
- miscellaneous
- nutritious
- outrageous
- prestigious
- rambunctious
- religious
- scrumptious
- spontaneous
- superstitious
- victorious

Focus

This week's focus is on multisyllabic words that end with *–ious* or *–eous*. When the *i* is preceded by *t*, the *ti* makes a /sh/ or /ch/ sound. When the suffix is preceded by *g*, the *ge* or *gi* makes a /j/ sound.

Helpful Hint

Notice that all the words on this list end with *–ious* or *–eous*. When *ti* appears before *–ous*, it makes a /sh/ sound (*ram·bunc·tious, nu·tri·tious*) unless it's preceded by *n* (*con·sci·en·tious*), in which case it makes a /ch/ sound. After most consonants, *i* makes a long *e* sound (*vic·tor·i·ous, hil·ar·i·ous*). The letter *i* is used to soften *g* in words (*re·li·gious, con·ta·gious*). Sometimes, *e* does the same job (*cour·a·geous, out·ra·geous*). At other times, *e* is pronounced as a separate syllable (*ig·ne·ous, spon·ta·ne·ous*).

See the Digital Resources for additional spelling activities.

Name: _____ **Date:** _____

Directions: Use a word from the Word Bank to complete each sentence.

Word Bank			
ambitious	anxious	gorgeous	igneous
miscellaneous	outrageous	prestigious	rambunctious
religious	spontaneous	superstitious	victorious

1. The actress wore a _____ sequined gown to the award show.

2. An _____ person sets lofty goals for herself and strives to achieve them.

3. My best friend loves to wear _____ outfits to school. Yesterday, she wore army boots, a pink tutu, and a basketball jersey!

4. Cameron was so _____ about getting a tooth pulled, he could barely sleep.

5. Mom keeps _____ items in her purse, such as tissues, candy, and a screwdriver.

6. The children were so _____ that Dad had to calm them down by turning on a movie.

7. Kimi has high SAT scores. She's applying to the most _____ colleges in the United States.

8. This wasn't a _____ decision. I've been planning to dye my hair purple for months!

9. My friends tease me about being _____ , but I know these mismatched socks bring me luck.

10. After a long, bloody battle at Gettysburg, Union forces were _____ against General Robert E. Lee.

11. My grandpa is extremely _____ . He goes to church three times a week.

12. Pumice, granite, and other types of _____ rock form when magma cools and hardens.

Name: _____ **Date:** _____

Directions: Use a word from the Word Bank for each section.

Word Bank			
anxious	cautious	contagious	courageous
hilarious	igneous	miscellaneous	nutritious
prestigious	rambunctious	scrumptious	spontaneous

Write a synonym for each word or phrase.

1. brave _____

2. assorted _____

3. very funny _____

4. rowdy _____

Write an antonym for each word or phrase.

5. carefully planned _____

6. careless _____

7. calm _____

8. unhealthy _____

Write a word that fits each category.

9. esteemed, admired, outstanding, _____

10. tasty, delicious, mouthwatering, _____

11. infectious, catching, communicable, _____

12. sedimentary, metamorphic, _____

Prefixes, Suffixes, and Roots

Name: _____ **Date:** _____

Directions: Did you know that *tact* and *tang* come from a Latin word that means *touch*? Use a word from the Word Bank to match each definition.

Word Bank			
contact	contagious	contiguous	contingent
intact	intangible	tact	tactful
tactile	tangent	tangible	tango

1. _____ able to be **touched** (*adjective*)

2. _____ not able to be **touched** (*adjective*)

3. _____ **touching** each other, such as all the states except Alaska and Hawaii (*adjective*)

4. _____ like a disease that can be spread by **touch** (*adjective*)

5. _____ get in **touch** with a person (*verb*)

6. _____ not damaged or broken; all the pieces are still **touching** (*adjective*)

7. _____ considerate; mindful of how one's actions **touch** or affect someone else (*adjective*)

8. _____ a sense of how one's actions **touch** or affect others (*noun*)

9. _____ related to the sense of **touch** (*adjective*)

10. _____ a different line of thought; a topic that doesn't **touch** what you were just talking about (*noun*)

11. _____ a type of dance that requires partners to **touch** by dancing cheek to cheek (*noun*)

12. _____ dependent on something else; **touched** by an action that will occur first (*adjective*)

Name: _____ **Date:** _____

Directions: Your school has just installed a new sound system for all its athletic fields. Students are now taking turns announcing games over the loudspeaker. It's your turn to be the announcer for the next big game. Write six comments you might make during the game. Use at least six of the *-ous* words.

Word Bank				
adventurous	anxious	cautious	courageous	dangerous
disastrous	enormous	fabulous	famous	hilarious
ludicrous	marvelous	miraculous	ominous	outrageous
perilous	ridiculous	spontaneous	tremendous	victorious

- _____
  _____

- _____
  _____

- _____
  _____

- _____
  _____

- _____
  _____

- _____
  _____

Here's the Scenario

Analogies

Name: _____ Date: _____

Directions: Use a word from the Word Bank to complete each analogy.

Word Bank			
ambitious	anxious	cautious	contagious
courageous	hilarious	igneous	nutritious
prestigious	religious	scrumptious	victorious

1. **candy** is to **unhealthy** as **vegetables** is to _____

2. **knight** is to **valiant** as **firefighter** is to _____

3. **coach** is to **encouraging** as **crossing guard** is to _____

4. **flag** is to **patriotic** as **cross** is to _____

5. **sandstone** is to **sedimentary** as **granite** is to _____

6. **before opening gifts** is to **excited** as **before taking a test** is to _____

7. **losing army** is to **defeated** as **winning army** is to _____

8. **essay** is to **reasonable** as **novel** is to _____

9. **allergies** is to **not spreadable** as **colds** is to _____

10. **burned toast** is to **unappetizing** as **gourmet meal** is to _____

11. **very sad** is to **heartbreaking** as **very funny** is to _____

12. **school spelling bee** is to **praiseworthy** as **National Spelling Bee** is to

_____

UNIT 30
More *ti* and *si* Patterns

Focus

This week's focus is on multisyllabic words that contain *ti* or *si*. When *ti* or *si* appear before a vowel suffix such as *–or, –ant*, or *–ous*, they make a /*sh*/ or /*ch*/ sound.

Helpful Hint

Notice that all the words on this list have *si* or *ti* before the suffix. When *si* appears before a suffix, it makes a /*sh*/ sound (*A·sian, con·tro·ver·sial*). When *ti* appears before a suffix, it also makes a /*sh*/ sound (*in·i·tial, pa·tient*). But if *n* precedes *ti*, it makes a /*ch*/ sound instead (*es·sen·tial, po·ten·tial*).

- Asian
- Christian
- confidential
- controversial
- credential
- essential
- influential
- initial
- initiative
- negotiate
- partial
- patience
- patient
- potential
- preferential
- quotient
- residential
- sequential
- substantial
- torrential

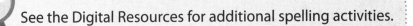

See the Digital Resources for additional spelling activities.

Name: _____ **Date:** _____

Directions: Use a word from the Word Bank to complete each sentence.

Word Bank			
controversial	credential	essential	influential
initiative	negotiate	partial	potential
preferential	residential	sequential	substantial

1. Camila needs _____ seating in the classroom because she has trouble seeing the board.

2. Ashton tried to _____ with his parents for a shorter punishment, but they said no.

3. Long division is a _____ method. If you do the steps out of order, you'll get the wrong answer.

4. Uncle Joe is a very _____ person in my life. I want to become a Navy SEAL just like him.

5. Large, loud trucks are discouraged from driving through _____ areas that are full of houses.

6. Mrs. Schaefer said she'll give us _____ credit if we show all our work but get the answer wrong.

7. Eggs are an _____ ingredient in any omelet, but cheese is optional.

8. The hurricane caused a _____ amount of damage to houses on the coastline. Some were uninhabitable.

9. The topic of school uniforms is _____ at my school. Students on both sides of the issue have strong opinions.

10. My teacher had to go to college to get a teaching _____ .

11. Mom makes me schedule my own dentist appointments so I can practice taking

    _____ .

12. Power tools have the _____ to cause serious injury if they're not used correctly.

Name: _____ **Date:** _____

Directions: Use a word from the Word Bank for each section.

Word Bank			
Asian	Christian	confidential	controversial
credential	essential	negotiate	partial
patience	residential	sequential	substantial

Write a synonym for each word or phrase.

1. necessary _____

2. private _____

3. arguable _____

4. bargain with _____

Write an antonym for each word.

5. random _____

6. frustration _____

7. whole _____

8. minor _____

Write a word that fits each category.

9. Muslim, Buddhist, Hindu, _____

10. African, European, Australian, _____

11. industrial, commercial, agricultural, _____

12. ID, documentation, qualification, _____

Name: _____ Date: _____

Directions: Did you know that the root *flu* comes from a Latin root that means *flow*? Use a word from the Word Bank to match each definition.

Prefixes, Suffixes, and Roots

Word Bank			
affluence	affluent	fluctuate	fluency
fluent	fluid	flush	flux
influence	influential	influx	reflux

1. _____ able to express oneself easily; able to make words **flow** (*adjective*)

2. _____ the ability to express oneself and make words **flow** (*noun*)

3. _____ rich, wealthy; having a steady **flow** of money (*adjective*)

4. _____ wealth; a steady **flow** of money (*noun*)

5. _____ a liquid; a substance that **flows** and takes the shape of its container (*noun*)

6. _____ rise and fall; **flow** up and down in an unpredictable way (*verb*)

7. _____ power to **flow** over someone; affecting or changing him or her in an important way (*noun*)

8. _____ able to **flow** over someone and affect or change him or her in an important way (*adjective*)

9. _____ cause a sudden **flow** of water in a toilet or pipe (*verb*)

10. _____ a continuous **flow**; a state of nonstop change (*noun*)

11. _____ the arrival or inward **flow** of many people or objects (*noun*)

12. _____ a medical condition in which stomach acid **flows** back up into the esophagus (*noun*)

Name: _____   Date:_____

Directions: Answer each question in a complete sentence. Remember to turn the question around, and use the bold word in your answer.

1. What are some **Asian** countries?

    _____

    _____

2. Why do kindergarten teachers need so much **patience**?

    _____

    _____

3. Why do some students require **preferential** seating in the classroom?

    _____

    _____

4. What are three items that are **essential** to have in a first aid kit?

    _____

    _____

5. Why is the speed limit lower in **residential** areas?

    _____

    _____

6. Do you think parents or classmates are more **influential** in a sixth grader's life? Explain.

    _____

    _____

Turn the Question Around

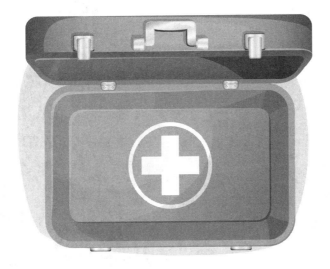

Name: _____ **Date:** _____

Directions: Use a word from the Word Bank to complete each analogy.

Word Bank			
Asian	Christian	confidential	controversial
essential	initial	negotiate	patient
quotient	residential	sequential	torrential

1. **teacher** is to **student** as **doctor** is to _____

2. **factories** is to **industrial** as **houses** is to _____

3. **train caboose** is to **final** as **train engine** is to _____

4. **France** is to **European** as **China** is to _____

5. **multiply** is to **product** as **divide** is to _____

6. **rain shower** is to **light** as **downpour** is to _____

7. **5, 92, 31** is to **random** as **4, 5, 6** is to _____

8. **golden rule** is to **widely accepted** as **capital punishment** is to _____

9. **Passover** is to **Jewish** as **Easter** is to _____

10. **job offer** is to **accept** as **contract** is to _____

11. **dessert** is to **optional** as **dinner** is to _____

12. **username** is to **public** as **password** is to _____

UNIT 31
qu Pattern

- acquaintance
- antique
- banquet
- bouquet
- boutique
- clique
- conquer
- critique
- croquet
- delinquent
- etiquette
- grotesque
- mosque
- oblique
- opaque
- picturesque
- plaque
- technique
- tourniquet
- unique

Focus

This week's focus is on *qu* words that have been influenced by the French language. The *–que* and *–quet* endings are introduced.

Helpful Hint

Notice that all the words on this list contain *qu*. The *qu* pattern is always followed by *e* when it appears at the end of a word (*antique*, *boutique*). The *–que* ending is found in many words that come from French. Words that end with *–quet* are also French. Some *–quet* words have retained their French pronunciation (*bouquet*, *croquet*), but others have been Anglicized to sound more like English words (*banquet*, *tourniquet*).

🔍 See the Digital Resources for additional spelling activities.

Name: _____ Date: _____

Directions: Use a word from the Word Bank to complete each sentence.

Word Bank			
banquet	boutique	clique	delinquent
etiquette	mosque	oblique	opaque
picturesque	plaque	technique	unique

1. Maya's _____ always sits near the cafeteria windows and refuses to let anyone join them.

2. We purchased _____ blinds for the bedroom window to block the bright morning sun.

3. Ricardo had a $27 late fee on his credit card bill because last month's payment was _____ .

4. What's the proper _____ for birthday parties? Should you invite friends a week in advance?

5. Abdullah went to the _____ to pray with his father on Friday.

6. Grandpa's fishing club presented him with a _____ to recognize his 20 years of service.

7. Chad found a website that allows you to design your own dirt bike. Every bike is _____ !

8. I received the Girl Scout Silver Award at our _____ , which was held at a local restaurant.

9. You might have trouble finding Grace's driveway since it meets the road at an _____ angle.

10. Sophie taught me a new, easier _____ for tie-dying T-shirts in the backyard.

11. We enjoyed a _____ drive through the Great Smoky Mountains on Sunday.

12. Let's stop at the new _____ that opened up on Main Street and see if they sell beagle socks.

Name: _____   Date: _____

Directions: Use a word from the Word Bank for each section.

Word Bank

acquaintance	antique	conquer	delinquent
etiquette	mosque	oblique	opaque
picturesque	plaque	technique	unique

Write a synonym for each word or phrase.

1. method _____
2. good manners _____
3. irresponsible _____
4. defeat _____

Write an antonym for each word.

5. modern _____
6. transparent _____
7. common _____
8. friend _____

Write a word that fits each category.

9. trophy, medal, certificate, _____
10. temple, church, synagogue, _____
11. vertical, horizontal, curved, _____
12. scenic, pretty, beautiful, _____

Synonyms and Antonyms

Name: _____ **Date:** _____

Directions: Did you know that the roots *cris* and *crit* come from a Latin word that means *separate* or *choose*? The root *tech* comes from a Greek word that means *skill* or *art*. Use a word from the Word Bank to match each definition.

Word Bank			
crisis	criteria	critic	critical
criticism	criticize	critique	hypocrite
technical	technician	technique	technology

1. _____ a person who strongly expresses his opinion and **chooses** sides on an issue (*noun*)

2. _____ likely to express one's opinions and **choose** sides on an issue (*adjective*)

3. _____ express disapproval or blame; make comments that **separate** oneself from the person or issue at fault (*verb*)

4. _____ disapproval or blame; comments that **separate** a person from the person or issue at fault (*noun*)

5. _____ the standards on which a judgment or **choice** may be made (*noun*)

6. _____ carefully study a behavior; **choose** strengths and weaknesses to discuss (*verb*)

7. _____ a person who claims to act one way but then **chooses** to act the opposite way (*noun*)

8. _____ an unstable or challenging time when difficult **choices** must be made (*noun*)

9. _____ a skillful way of doing something, especially an **artistic** or scientific task (*noun*)

10. _____ relating to a particular **art** or **skill** (*adjective*)

11. _____ the study of problems and their solutions, achieved by creating new tools or **skills** (*noun*)

12. _____ a person who has specialized skills in an **art** or scientific field (*noun*)

Prefixes, Suffixes, and Roots

Name: _____ **Date:** _____

Directions: Answer each question in a complete sentence. Remember to turn the question around, and use the bold word in your answer.

1. What happens if a person is **delinquent** in paying his or her credit card bill?

   _____

   _____

2. If you could open any kind of **boutique**, what would you sell there?

   _____

   _____

3. Why are **cliques** a problem in elementary and middle school?

   _____

   _____

4. Why would you apply a **tourniquet** to someone's arm or leg?

   _____

   _____

5. Do you like to have people **critique** your writing? Explain.

   _____

   _____

6. What is your **technique** for making a bed?

   _____

   _____

Name: _____ Date:_____

Directions: Use a word from the Word Bank to complete each analogy.

Word Bank			
antique	bouquet	boutique	clique
conquer	croquet	grotesque	mosque
oblique	opaque	plaque	tourniquet

1. **group of birds** is to **flock** as **group of friends** is to _____

2. **minor bleeding** is to **bandage** as **major bleeding** is to _____

3. **Christian** is to **church** as **Muslim** is to _____

4. **large selection** is to **department store** as **small selection** is to _____

5. **plastic wrap** is to **transparent** as **wax paper** is to _____

6. **flowers in soil** is to **garden** as **flowers in hand** is to _____

7. **shelf** is to **trophy** as **wall** is to _____

8. **princess** is to **beautiful** as **ogre** is to _____

9. **club** is to **golf** as **mallet** is to _____

10. **new lamps** is to **modern** as **old lamps** is to _____

11. **parenthesis** is to **curved** as **backslash** is to _____

12. **obstacles** is to **overcome** as **fears** is to _____

UNIT 32
More Soft G Words

Focus

This week's focus is on multisyllabic words that contain soft *g*. Soft *g* is always followed by *e, i,* or *y.*

Helpful Hint

Notice that each word on this list has a soft *g* sound in one of its syllables. Soft *g* is always followed by *e, i,* or *y.* Many words are derived from the Latin roots *leg* and *lig,* which can mean *law* or *select.* The *g* in these roots can have a hard or soft pronunciation, depending on which letter comes next (*negligent, legislature, elegant, delegate*).

See the Digital Resources for additional spelling activities.

- agility
- allegiance
- allergen
- congenital
- detergent
- digital
- diligent
- generic
- generosity
- geometry
- indulgent
- legendary
- legislature
- manageable
- negligent
- nostalgic
- prodigious
- pungent
- regional
- strategy

Sentence Completions

Name: _____   Date:_____

Directions: Use a word from the Word Bank to complete each sentence.

Word Bank			
agility	allegiance	allergen	congenital
digital	generic	indulgent	negligent
nostalgic	prodigious	pungent	strategy

1. Every morning at school, we pledge _____ to the flag and our country, the United States.

2. Our local library has a _____ collection of children's picture books. There are 10,000!

3. Kai's parents were too _____ , so now he has tantrums every time someone says no to him.

4. Texting while driving is _____ behavior because it can cause you to hurt or kill someone.

5. The _____ that causes me to sneeze the most is pollen. Spring is a tough time for me!

6. My baby cousin needed surgery due to a _____ heart problem.

7. We need a new _____ for scoring baskets. Our usual plays are not working.

8. Mom asked the pharmacist if a cheaper _____ brand was available for my prescription.

9. There's a _____ odor coming from the laundry room. It smells gross, like sour milk!

10. Tennis requires _____ since you're constantly moving your feet and switching directions.

11. The smell of apple pie always makes me _____ and reminds me of Thanksgiving at Gram's.

12. Ava never learned how to tell time because all the clocks in her house were

    _____ .

Name: _____   Date: _____

Directions: Use a word from the Word Bank for each section.

Word Bank			
allegiance	congenital	detergent	diligent
generic	generosity	indulgent	negligent
nostalgic	prodigious	pungent	strategy

Write a synonym for each word or phrase.

1. hardworking _____

2. careless _____

3. since birth _____

4. loyalty _____

Write an antonym for each word or phrase.

5. brand-name _____

6. strict _____

7. small and unimpressive _____

8. fragrant _____

9. stinginess _____

Write a word that fits each category.

10. sentimental, homesick, longing for the past, _____

11. soap, cleaner, stain remover, _____

12. plan, method, scheme, _____

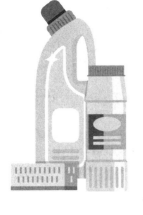   

Name: _____ Date: _____

Directions: Did you know that the root *leg* comes from a Latin word that means *law*? The *leg* and *lig* roots also come from a similar Latin word that means *select* or *choose*. Use a word from the Word Bank to match each definition.

Word Bank			
delegate	diligent	elegant	eligible
illegal	intelligent	legal	legislator
legislature	legitimate	negligent	privilege

1. _____ **lawful** (*adjective*)

2. _____ not **lawful** (*adjective*)

3. _____ the branch of government that makes **laws** (*noun*)

4. _____ a senator, representative, or congressperson; someone who makes **laws** (*noun*)

5. _____ genuine, real, or **lawful** (*adjective*)

6. _____ a special benefit or right; something that bends the **law** in one's favor (*noun*)

7. _____ assign tasks; **select** different jobs for each person that is working with you (*verb*)

8. _____ hardworking; **choosing** to put your best effort into a task (*adjective*)

9. _____ careless; **choosing** not to keep your children or property safe (*adjective*)

10. _____ pleasingly graceful and stylish; skilled at making tasteful **choices** (*adjective*)

11. _____ able to be **selected** for a team or position (*adjective*)

12. _____ smart; able to **select**, retain, and express appropriate information (*adjective*)

28634—180 Days of Spelling and Word Study © *Shell Education*

Prefixes, Suffixes, and Roots

Name: _____ **Date:** _____

Directions: Write 10 of the words from the Word Bank two times each in your best cursive.

Word Bank				
agility	allegiance	allergen	congenital	detergent
digital	diligent	generic	generosity	geometry
indulgent	legendary	legislature	manageable	negligent
nostalgic	prodigious	pungent	regional	strategy

_____ _____

_____ _____

_____ _____

_____ _____

_____ _____

_____ _____

_____ _____

_____ _____

_____ _____

Analogies

Name: _____ Date: _____

Directions: Use a word from the Word Bank to complete each analogy.

Word Bank			
agility	allergen	detergent	digital
geometry	indulgent	legendary	legislature
manageable	nostalgic	pungent	regional

1. **dirty hair** is to **shampoo** as **dirty clothes** is to _____

2. **millions, tenths** is to **place value** as **triangles, squares** is to _____

3. **sick** is to **germ** as **allergic** is to _____

4. **in one state** is to **statewide** as **in neighboring states** is to _____

5. **distance race** is to **stamina** as **hurdle race** is to _____

6. **fresh flowers** is to **fragrant** as **garbage** is to _____

7. **hope for the future** is to **optimistic** as **long for the past** is to _____

8. is to **analog** as  is to _____

9. **Supreme Court** is to **judiciary** as **Congress** is to _____

10. **eight hours of homework** is to **excessive** as **one hour of homework** is to

    _____

11. **parents who set limits** is to **strict** as **parents who don't set limits** is to

    _____

12. **Adolf Hitler** is to **infamous** as **Abe Lincoln** is to _____

UNIT 33
ph Words

Focus

This week's focus is on multisyllabic words that contain the *ph* digraph. The *ph* pattern is found in many Greek roots, such as *graph* and *photo*.

Helpful Hint

Notice that each word on this list contains a *ph* pattern that sounds like /f/. The *ph* pattern can be found in common Greek roots, such as *photo (photocopy, photosynthesis), graph (geography, biography),* and *soph (philosophy, sophomore, sophisticated).*

- ➤ **amphibian**
- ➤ **apostrophe**
- ➤ **biography**
- ➤ **catastrophe**
- ➤ **decipher**
- ➤ **esophagus**
- ➤ **geography**
- ➤ **metamorphosis**
- ➤ **peripheral**
- ➤ **pharmacist**
- ➤ **phenomenon**
- ➤ **philosophy**
- ➤ **photocopy**
- ➤ **photographer**
- ➤ **photosynthesis**
- ➤ **physical**
- ➤ **sophisticated**
- ➤ **sophomore**
- ➤ **triumphant**
- ➤ **xylophone**

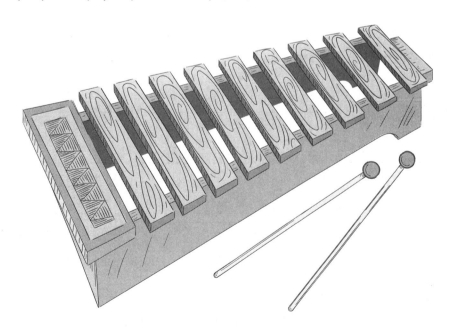

🔍 See the Digital Resources for additional spelling activities.

Sentence Completions

Name: _____ Date: _____

Directions: Use a word from the Word Bank to complete each sentence.

Word Bank			
apostrophe	catastrophe	decipher	esophagus
metamorphosis	peripheral	phenomenon	philosophy
photosynthesis	sophisticated	sophomore	triumphant

1. Families were _____ when the board announced it would keep their school open.

2. In Iceland, you can witness an amazing _____ in the sky called the Northern Lights.

3. Mom bought my little brother a butterfly house so he could watch the caterpillars' _____ .

4. Don't forget to add an _____ when you write contractions, such as *let's* and *you're*.

5. Don't wear a hood when you ride your bike because it might block your _____ vision.

6. Sahara took the PSAT for the first time when she was a _____ in high school.

7. I could feel the hot soup burning my _____ as it traveled down to my stomach.

8. The hurricane was the deadliest and most expensive _____ to strike the island nation.

9. Bradley jotted down the recipe for me, but I can't _____ most of the words.

10. Now that my sister's in middle school, she acts like she's so much more _____ than I am.

11. My parents' _____ is that children need lots of time to run around and play outside.

12. Does _____ occur all year, or do plants only make food during the summer months?

Name: _____   **Date:** _____

Directions: Use a word from the Word Bank for each section.

Synonyms and Antonyms

Word Bank			
amphibian	apostrophe	catastrophe	decipher
esophagus	metamorphosis	peripheral	pharmacist
phenomenon	sophisticated	sophomore	triumphant

Write a synonym for each word or phrase.

1. disaster _____

2. on the edge _____

3. victorious _____

4. significant
   or rare event _____

Write an antonym for each word or phrase.

5. encode _____

6. naive _____

7. drugstore
   customer _____

Write a word that fits each category.

8. mammal, fish, reptile, _____

9. quotation mark, comma, period, _____

10. stomach, small intestine, large intestine, _____

11. senior, freshman, junior, _____

12. change, transformation, life cycle, _____

Name: _____ **Date:** _____

Directions: Did you know that the root *photo* comes from a Greek word that means *light*? The root *soph* comes from a Greek word that means *wisdom*. Use a word from the Word Bank to match each definition.

Word Bank

philosopher	philosophical	philosophy	photocopy
photogenic	photograph	photographer	photography
photosynthesis	sophisticated	sophomore	unsophisticated

1. _____ take pictures by allowing **light** to pass through the lens of a camera (*verb*)

2. _____ the process of taking pictures by allowing **light** to pass through a lens (*noun*)

3. _____ a person who takes pictures by allowing **light** to pass through a lens (*noun*)

4. _____ attractive; describing a person who usually looks good in photos (*adjective*)

5. _____ duplicate; use **light** rays in a machine to copy a printed document (*verb*)

6. _____ a plant's way of using **light** to make food (*noun*)

7. _____ a second-year high school or college student; one who attends school to pursue **wisdom** (*noun*)

8. _____ the pursuit of **wisdom**; the study of life's big questions and answers (*noun*)

9. _____ a person who pursues **wisdom** by attempting to ask and answer life's big questions (*noun*)

10. _____ pursuing **wisdom**; curious and thoughtful about life's big questions and answers (*adjective*)

11. _____ knowledgeable about culture, art, and literature; **wise** due to life experiences (*adjective*)

12. _____ lacking knowledge about culture, art, and literature, not **wise** about the world (*adjective*)

Name: _____ **Date:** _____

Directions: Answer each question in a complete sentence. Remember to turn the question around, and use the bold word in your answer.

1. What are the stages of a butterfly's **metamorphosis**?

   _____

   _____

2. What is the purpose of an **apostrophe**?

   _____

   _____

3. Why is it important for drivers to have good **peripheral** vision?

   _____

   _____

4. Why do people get so excited about rainbows and other natural **phenomena**?

   _____

   _____

5. What are some characteristics of **amphibians**?

   _____

   _____

6. When was a time you felt **triumphant**?

   _____

   _____

Analogies

Name: _____ **Date:** _____

Directions: Use a word from the Word Bank to complete each analogy.

Word Bank			
amphibian	apostrophe	biography	catastrophe
decipher	geography	pharmacist	photocopy
photographer	physical	sophomore	xylophone

1.   **ninth grade** is to **freshman** as **tenth grade** is to _____

2.   **snake** is to **reptile** as **toad** is to _____

3.   **study of weather** is to **meteorology** as **study of Earth** is to _____

4.   **show dialogue** is to **quotation marks** as **show ownership** is to _____

5.   **writer's life story** is to **autobiography** as **someone else's story** is to _____

6.   **person** is to **photograph** as **document** is to _____

7.   **of the mind** is to **mental** as **of the body** is to _____

8.   **keys** is to **piano** as **bars** is to _____

9.   **draw pictures** is to **artist** as **take pictures** is to _____

10.   **surprise** is to **bombshell** as **problem** is to _____

11.   **foreign language** is to **translate** as **secret code** is to _____

12.   **fill orders** is to **warehouse worker** as **fill prescriptions** is to _____

28634—180 Days of Spelling and Word Study   © *Shell Education*

UNIT 34
More Soft C Patterns

Focus

This week's focus is on multisyllabic words that contain soft *c*. Soft *c* is always followed by *e, i,* or *y*.

Helpful Hint

Notice that each word on this list has a soft *c* sound in one of its syllables. Soft *c* is always followed by *e, i,* or *y*. In *double c* words, such as *accentuate*, *accessible*, and *eccentric*, the first *c* is hard and the second *c* is soft. In words such as *scientific* and *descendant*, the *s* is silent and the *c* is soft.

See the Digital Resources for additional spelling activities.

- accentuate
- accessible
- accidentally
- adolescent
- celebration
- celebrity
- circumstances
- coincidence
- condescending
- convalescent
- descendant
- eccentric
- fascination
- fluorescent
- necessary
- publicity
- reminisce
- scientific
- succinctly
- susceptible

Name: _____ **Date:** _____

Directions: Use a word from the Word Bank to complete each sentence.

Word Bank			
accentuate	accessible	circumstances	coincidence
condescending	convalescent	descendant	eccentric
fascination	publicity	reminisce	susceptible

1. My mom researched our family tree and found out she is a _____ of Ben Franklin!

2. People who burn easily are more _____ to skin cancer.

3. On Christmas Eve, we _____ about past holidays.

4. I would like to be famous, but I wouldn't like the _____ .

5. My brother acts superior and speaks to me in a _____ tone.

6. My neighbor lives in a purple house with 12 cats. He's very _____!

7. We'll need to build a ramp and widen the front door to make our house _____ to Jordie and her wheelchair.

8. What a _____! Alicia, Ben, and I all went to the orthodontist to get braces on the same day.

9. Aunt Barbara will have to stay at a _____ home for a few weeks until her broken hip heals.

10. Due to unforeseen _____ , we have to cancel tonight's concert and reschedule it for Tuesday.

11. Peter's _____ with trains started when he was three and visited the Trolley Museum.

12. My sister only wears colors that _____ her pretty green eyes.

Name: _____ **Date:** _____

Directions: Use a word from the Word Bank for each section.

Word Bank			
accentuate	accessible	accidentally	adolescent
celebrity	descendant	eccentric	necessary
publicity	reminisce	succinctly	susceptible

Write a synonym for each word or phrase.

1. remember
   the past _____

2. teenager _____

3. reachable _____

4. required _____

Write an antonym for each word or phrase.

5. conceal _____

6. ancestor _____

7. on purpose _____

8. immune _____

Write a word that fits each category.

9. odd, strange, unusual, _____

10. briefly, concisely, with few words, _____

11. advertising, attention, public interest, _____

12. star, famous person, legend, _____

Name: _____ **Date:** _____

Directions: The *esce* root comes from a Latin suffix that means *become*. The *scend* root comes from a Latin word that means *climb*. The *cide* root can mean *happen* or *fall into*. Use a word from the Word Bank to match each definition.

<table>
<tr><td colspan="4">**Word Bank**</td></tr>
<tr><td>accident</td><td>accidentally</td><td>adolescent</td><td>ascend</td></tr>
<tr><td>coincidence</td><td>coincidentally</td><td>condescending</td><td>convalescent</td></tr>
<tr><td>descend</td><td>descendant</td><td>fluorescent</td><td>incident</td></tr>
</table>

1. _____ a person who is **becoming** healthy again after an illness or injury (*noun*)

2. _____ a teenager; a person who is **becoming** an adult (*noun*)

3. _____ **becoming** bright or colorful, such as markers or overhead lighting (*adjective*)

4. _____ **climb** up (*verb*)

5. _____ **climb** down (*verb*)

6. _____ a person who is related to someone from an earlier generation; a relative of someone who is a higher **climb** up the family tree (*noun*)

7. _____ having a superior attitude; acting like one has to **climb** down a few social levels to interact with a person (*adjective*)

8. _____ something that does not **happen** on purpose (*noun*)

9. _____ **happening** unexpectedly or by chance; not **happening** on purpose (ad*verb*)

10. _____ something that **happens** and seems minor but can lead to major consequences (*noun*)

11. _____ two things that randomly **happen** at the same time but somehow seem related (*noun*)

12. _____ **happening** randomly at the same time while seeming somehow related (ad*verb*)

Prefixes, Suffixes, and Roots

Name: _____ **Date:** _____

Directions: Read each idiom or proverb, and write a sentence explaining its meaning.

1. **Practice** what you preach.

   _____

   _____

   _____

2. Honesty is the best **policy**.

   _____

   _____

   _____

3. Laughter is the best **medicine**.

   _____

   _____

   _____

4. **Success** has many fathers, while failure is an orphan.

   _____

   _____

   _____

An **idiom** is an expression that is widely used but shouldn't be taken literally. An example is, "It's raining cats and dogs." A **proverb** is a short saying that offers advice. An example is, "Two wrongs don't make a right."

Analogies

Name: _____ **Date:** _____

Directions: Use a word from the Word Bank to complete each analogy.

Word Bank

accentuate	adolescent	celebration	circumstance
coincidence	convalescent	descendant	fluorescent
necessary	reminisce	scientific	susceptible

1. **2 years old** is to **toddler** as **14 years old** is to _____

2. **before** is to **ancestor** as **after** is to _____

3. **baby blue** is to **pastel** as **hot pink** is to _____

4. **future** is to **imagine** as **past** is to _____

5. **funeral** is to **somber** as **wedding** is to _____

6. **during surgery** is to **patient** as **after surgery** is to _____

7. **flaw** is to **hide** as **best feature** is to _____

8. **doesn't get sick** is to **immune** as **gets sick easily** is to _____

9. **governor** is to **political** as **chemist** is to _____

10. **at the park** is to **location** as **in the rain** is to _____

11. **decals on a bike** is to **optional** as **brakes on a bike** is to _____

12. **see friend at school** is to **planned** as **see friend at the store** is to _____

UNIT 35
Hard *ch* Words

Focus

This week's focus is on multisyllabic words that contain the *ch* digraph. In each word, *ch* makes a /k/ sound.

Helpful Hint

Notice that every word on this list has a *ch* pattern that sounds like /k/. The hard *ch* pattern is found in many words that come from Greek. *Arch* (chief) and *chron* (time) are two Greek roots that you'll explore in this unit.

- arachnid
- architect
- archives
- bronchitis
- chameleon
- chaos
- character
- characteristics
- charisma
- chemical
- chemistry
- choreograph
- chronic
- chronological
- chrysalis
- mechanic
- monarch
- orchestra
- scholarship
- technical

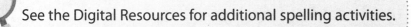

See the Digital Resources for additional spelling activities.

Name: _____ **Date:** _____

Directions: Use a word from the Word Bank to complete each sentence.

Word Bank			
architect	archives	chaos	characteristics
charisma	chemical	choreograph	chronic
chronological	monarch	scholarship	technical

1. George and I researched and wrote the _____ of different breeds of dogs.

2. Olivia and I are going to _____ a dance so we can perform it at the talent show.

3. Scientists have developed new medications to treat _____ diseases, such as asthma and diabetes.

4. We experienced _____ difficulties when we tried to project our video clip onto the screen.

5. When the power went out at the mall, _____ erupted.

6. King Charles II was England's _____ during the Great Plague of 1665.

7. People have always been drawn to Tyler because of his charming smile and

   _____ .

8. I found an old document in the _____ of the city library.

9. When you summarize a story, you need to retell the most important events in

   _____ order.

10. The school board hired an _____ to draw up plans for a new elementary school.

11. Samuel earned a full _____ to college because of his impressive grades and test scores.

12. We had to wear gloves to protect ourselves from the _____ we were using in the experiment.

Name: _____ **Date:** _____

Directions: Use a word from the Word Bank for each section.

Word Bank

arachnid	bronchitis	chameleon	chaos
character	characteristics	charisma	choreograph
chronic	chronological	scholarship	technical

Write a synonym for each word or phrase.

1. disorder and confusion _____

2. spider _____

3. traits _____

4. referring to specialized knowledge _____

Write an antonym for each word or phrase.

5. not in order _____

6. lack of charm or appeal _____

7. short-term _____

Write a word that fits each category.

8. strep throat, ear infection, stomach bug, _____

9. setting, problem, solution, _____

10. loan, grant, award, _____

11. lizard, gecko, iguana, _____

12. plan, design, arrange, _____

Name: _____ Date:_____

Directions: Did you know that the root *chron* comes from a Greek word that means *time*? The root *arch* comes from a Greek word that means *chief* or *most important*. Use a word from the Word Bank to match each definition.

Word Bank			
anarchy	architect	archive	chronic
chronicle	chronological	chronology	hierarchy
matriarch	monarch	patriarch	synchronize

1. _____ make two things happen at the same **time** (*verb*)

2. _____ a way of organizing events by **time**, in the order they happened (*noun*)

3. _____ organized by **time**, in the order events happened (*adjective*)

4. _____ long-term; happening again and again over **time** (*adjective*)

5. _____ a record of events that happened over **time** (*noun*)

6. _____ a king or queen; the **most important** person in a kingdom (*noun*)

7. _____ the female head, or **chief**, of a family (*noun*)

8. _____ the male head, or **chief**, of a family (*noun*)

9. _____ the **chief** designer of a building (*noun*)

10. _____ disorder and craziness because there's no **chief** or person in charge (*noun*)

11. _____ a ranking system in which people or objects are listed by **importance** (*noun*)

12. _____ a place where **important** historical documents are preserved and displayed (*noun*)

Name: _____ Date:_____

Directions: Answer each question in a complete sentence. Remember to turn the question around, and use the bold word in your answer.

1. What are three **chronic** diseases a person might suffer from?

   _____

   _____

2. What is a merit **scholarship**?

   _____

   _____

3. Why do people visit the National **Archives**?

   _____

   _____

4. What are some **characteristics** of a superhero?

   _____

   _____

5. What do you know about **monarch** butterflies?

   _____

   _____

6. Would you rather be an **architect** or a **mechanic**? Explain.

   _____

   _____

Analogies

Name: _____ **Date:** _____

Directions: Use a word from the Word Bank to complete each analogy.

Word Bank			
arachnid	architect	archive	character
chemistry	choreograph	chronological	chrysalis
mechanic	monarch	orchestra	scholarship

1. **science of living things** is to **biology** as **science of substances** is to _____

2. **six legs** is to **insect** as **eight legs** is to _____

3. **build houses** is to **contractor** as **design houses** is to _____

4. **borrowed money** is to **loan** as **awarded money** is to _____

5. **sell cars** is to **dealer** as **fix cars** is to _____

6. **moth** is to **cocoon** as **caterpillar** is to _____

7. **do dance moves** is to **perform** as **plan dance moves** is to _____

8. **drums and guitars** is to **band** as **violins and cellos** is to _____

9. **first, second, third** is to **sequential** as **first, next, last** is to _____

10. **nonfiction** is to **historical figure** as **fiction** is to _____

11. **paintings** is to **museum** as **historical documents** is to _____

12. **republic** is to **president** as **kingdom** is to _____

UNIT 36
Soft *ch* Words

Focus

This week's focus is on multisyllabic words that contain the *ch* digraph. In each word, *ch* makes a /sh/ sound.

Helpful Hint

Notice that every word on this list has a *ch* pattern that sounds like /sh/. The soft *ch* pattern is found in many words that come from French.

- brochure
- chagrin
- chalet
- chandelier
- chaperone
- charade
- chauffeur
- chef
- Chicago
- chiffon
- chivalrous
- cliché
- crochet
- fuchsia
- machinery
- Michigan
- mustache
- nonchalant
- pistachio
- quiche

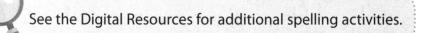

See the Digital Resources for additional spelling activities.

Name: _____ **Date:** _____

Directions: Use a word from the Word Bank to complete each sentence.

Word Bank			
brochure	chagrin	chalet	chandelier
chaperone	charade	chiffon	chivalrous
cliché	fuchsia	nonchalant	quiche

1. My mom offered to _____ our field trip to Washington, DC.

2. Giving up your seat on the subway for an elderly passenger is a kind and _____ act.

3. Marisa acted so _____ when the boys started teasing her, as if she couldn't even hear them.

4. I know it's a _____ , but the best things in life really are free.

5. The bridesmaids wore deep purple gowns that were made of a flowy _____ fabric.

6. Let's remember to pick up a _____ for a local attraction when we stop at the rest area.

7. Simon invited us to spend the weekend at his ski _____ on Mount Snow.

8. Much to my _____ , the birthday package was squashed by the post office.

9. Rebecca wants to use her favorite colors, turquoise and _____ , on her wedding day.

10. I learned how to make a _____ in my cooking class!

11. It took Dad two hours to clean the crystal _____ in Grandma's dining room.

12. You can quit the _____ . I know you're only pretending to be asleep!

Name: _____ Date: _____

Directions: Use a word from the Word Bank for each section.

Word Bank			
brochure	chagrin	chalet	chandelier
chauffeur	chef	chiffon	chivalrous
cliché	Michigan	nonchalant	pistachio

Write a synonym for each word or phrase.

1. annoyance
caused by failure
or disappointment _____

2. driver _____

3. overused
phrase _____

4. pamphlet _____

Write an antonym for each word or phrase.

5. rude _____

6. restaurant
guest _____

Write a word that fits each category.

7. carefree, unconcerned, not bothered or worried, _____

8. Minnesota, Wisconsin, Illinois, _____

9. cabin, lodge, cottage, _____

10. floor lamp, table lamp, light fixture, _____

11. satin, lace, tulle, _____

12. pecan, walnut, cashew, _____

Name: _____ **Date:** _____

Directions: Did you know that *card* comes from a Latin word that means *heart*, *corp* comes from a Latin word that means *body*, and *derm* comes from a Latin word that means *skin*? Use a word from the Word Bank to match each definition.

Word Bank			
cardiac	cardiologist	cardiology	corporate
corporation	dermatologist	dermatology	epidermis
incorporate	pachyderm		

1. _____ the study and treatment of **skin** disorders (*noun*)

2. _____ a doctor who studies and treats **skin** disorders (*noun*)

3. _____ the outer layer of **skin** (*noun*)

4. _____ a thick-**skinned** animal with hooves, such as an elephant or rhino (*noun*)

5. _____ the study and treatment of **heart** disorders (*noun*)

6. _____ a doctor who studies and treats **heart** disorders (*noun*)

7. _____ related to or affecting the **heart** (*adjective*)

8. _____ a business or company that has the rights and duties of one large **body** (*noun*)

9. _____ referring to a business or company that has the rights and duties of one large **body** (*adjective*)

10. _____ combine or blend parts to make one large **body** or whole (*verb*)

Name: _____   **Date:** _____

Directions: Answer each question in a complete sentence. Remember to turn the question around, and use the bold word in your answer.

1. What do visitors like to do in **Chicago**?

    _____

    _____

2. Why are parents invited to **chaperone** field trips?

    _____

    _____

3. What information should be included in a school **brochure**?

    _____

    _____

4. Why do authors try to avoid **clichés** in their writing?

    _____

    _____

5. Why would a mom act **nonchalant** when her four-year-old falls and cuts her knee?

    _____

    _____

6. Why do workers wear safety gear when they operate heavy **machinery**?

    _____

    _____

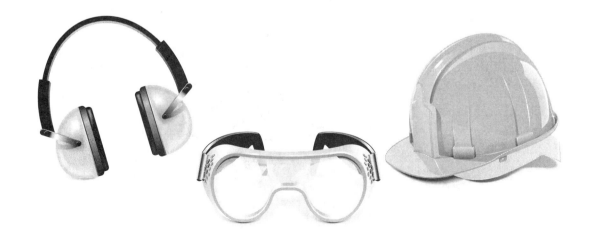

Analogies

Name: _____ **Date:** _____

Directions: Use a word from the Word Bank to complete each analogy.

Word Bank			
brochure	chandelier	chaperone	chauffeur
chef	Chicago	cliché	crochet
fuchsia	Michigan	mustache	pistachio

1. **shape** is to **square** as **color** is to _____

2. **California** is to **Los Angeles** as **Illinois** is to _____

3. **Southeast** is to **Florida** as **Midwest** is to _____

4. **classroom** is to **teacher** as **field trip** is to _____

5. **taxi** is to **cab driver** as **limousine** is to _____

6. **lower lip** is to **beard** as **upper lip** is to _____

7. **casual lighting** is to **floor lamp** as **fancy lighting** is to _____

8. **local streets** is to **map** as **local attractions** is to _____

9. **serves dinner** is to **waiter** as **prepares dinner** is to _____

10. **light as sea foam** is to **original simile** as **light as a feather** is to _____

11. **fruit** is to **apple** as **nut** is to _____

12. **thread** is to **embroider** as **yarn** is to _____

Answer Key (cont.)

Week 8 Day 5 (page 58)

1. sediment
2. advertisement
3. amendment
4. environment
5. settlement
6. measurement
7. excitement
8. implement
9. disagreement
10. announcement
11. disappointment
12. development

Week 9 Day 1 (page 60)

1. primitive
2. competitive
3. executive
4. extensive
5. alternative
6. adhesive
7. consecutive
8. representative
9. excessive
10. assertive
11. decorative
12. figurative

Week 9 Day 2 (page 61)

1. assertive
2. consecutive
3. adhesive
4. comprehensive
5. competitive
6. figurative
7. destructive
8. excessive
9. executive
10. informative
11. alternative
12. primitive

Week 9 Day 3 (page 62)

1. progress
2. progression
3. regress
4. digress
5. egress
6. aggression
7. aggressive
8. congress
9. transgression
10. gradual
11. grade
12. graduate

Week 9 Day 4 (page 63)

Responses must include bolded words.

Week 9 Day 5 (page 64)

1. possessive
2. decorative
3. executive
4. cooperative
5. consecutive
6. competitive
7. aggressive
8. informative
9. excessive
10. destructive
11. interactive
12. figurative

Week 10 Day 1 (page 66)

1. realtor
2. particular
3. muscular
4. ambassador
5. pioneer
6. denominator
7. escalator
8. engineer
9. competitor
10. investor
11. career
12. caterpillar

Week 10 Day 2 (page 67)

1. competitor
2. particular
3. career
4. muscular
5. investor
6. educator
7. denominator
8. alligator
9. refrigerator
10. elevator
11. engineer
12. ambassador

Week 10 Day 3 (page 68)

1. conductor
2. educator
3. education
4. abduct
5. reduce
6. reduction
7. introduce
8. produce
9. productive
10. aqueduct
11. duct
12. deduce

Week 10 Day 4 (page 69)

Answers should be a paragraph and use a minimum of six –er and –or words.

Week 10 Day 5 (page 70)

1. pioneers
2. professor
3. calculator
4. refrigerator
5. denominator
6. escalator
7. realtor
8. illustrator
9. competitor
10. investor
11. alligator
12. ambassador

Week 11 Day 1 (page 72)

1. expiration
2. transformation
3. exploration
4. preservation
5. inspiration
6. invitation
7. conservation
8. presentation
9. imagination
10. reservation
11. cancellation
12. declaration

Week 11 Day 2 (page 73)

1. perspiration
2. expiration
3. declaration
4. conservation
5. organization
6. admiration
7. transformation
8. cancellation
9. reservation
10. conversation
11. inspiration
12. combination

Week 11 Day 3 (page 74)

1. inhale
2. exhale
3. inhaler
4. expire
5. respiration
6. respiratory
7. inspire
8. inspiration
9. aspire
10. conspire
11. conspiracy
12. perspire

Week 11 Day 4 (page 75)

1. *Actions speak louder than words:* What you do is more important than what you say. Your actions show your true intentions and feelings.
2. *An ounce of prevention is worth a pound of cure:* It is better to stop a problem before it happens than wait and fix it later.
3. *Imitation is the sincerest form of flattery:* People copy you because they admire and want to be like you.
4. *Genius is one percent inspiration, ninety-nine percent perspiration:* Great accomplishments are the result of hard work, not a quick and easy idea.

Week 11 Day 5 (page 76)

1. perspiration
2. transportation
3. observation
4. cancellation
5. information
6. invitation
7. organization
8. reservation
9. expiration
10. conversation
11. declaration
12. transformation

Week 12 Day 1 (page 78)

1. resolution
2. legislation
3. notification
4. inauguration
5. application
6. recreation
7. institution
8. unification
9. constitution
10. decoration
11. Revolution
12. investigation

Answer Key *(cont.)*

Week 12 Day 2 (page 79)

1. recreation
2. investigation
3. congratulations
4. multiplication
5. evaporation
6. solution
7. legislation
8. decorations
9. institution
10. qualification
11. revolution
12. notification

Week 12 Day 3 (page 80)

1. grateful
2. ungrateful
3. gratitude
4. gratifying
5. gratification
6. gratuity
7. congratulate
8. congratulations
9. grace
10. graceful
11. gracious
12. disgrace

Week 12 Day 4 (page 81)

Responses must include bolded words.

Week 12 Day 5 (page 82)

1. evaporation
2. decorations
3. abbreviation
4. qualifications
5. congratulations
6. resolution
7. legislation
8. communication
9. inauguration
10. recreation
11. multiplication
12. investigation

Week 13 Day 1 (page 84)

1. apprehension
2. progression
3. precision
4. persuasion
5. procession
6. obsession
7. suspension
8. aggression
9. illusion
10. excursion
11. diversion
12. commission

Week 13 Day 2 (page 85)

1. incision
2. procession
3. excursion
4. apprehension
5. supervision
6. aggression
7. depression
8. obsession
9. provisions
10. diversion
11. commission
12. concessions

Week 13 Day 3 (page 86)

1. incisor
2. incision
3. scissors
4. excise
5. decide
6. decision
7. indecisive
8. concise
9. precise
10. imprecise
11. precision
12. pesticide

Week 13 Day 4 (page 87)

Answers should be a paragraph and use a minimum of six *–sion* words.

Week 13 Day 5 (page 88)

1. commission
2. concessions
3. television
4. depression
5. concussion
6. incision
7. suspension
8. excursion
9. provisions
10. procession
11. comprehension
12. precision

Week 14 Day 1 (page 90)

1. reasonable
2. perishable
3. noticeable
4. comparable
5. inevitable
6. manageable
7. comfortable
8. probable
9. charitable
10. irritable
11. vulnerable
12. variables

Week 14 Day 2 (page 91)

1. irritable
2. inevitable
3. vulnerable
4. comparable
5. charitable
6. probable
7. knowledgeable
8. undependable
9. noticeable
10. comfortable
11. remarkable
12. unbelievable

Week 14 Day 3 (page 92)

1. pendulum
2. pendant
3. depend
4. dependable
5. undependable
6. dependent
7. independent
8. suspend
9. suspenders
10. suspension
11. pending
12. impending

Week 14 Day 4 (page 93)

Responses must include bolded words.

Week 14 Day 5 (page 94)

1. comfortable
2. noticeable
3. perishable
4. unbelievable
5. vulnerable
6. inevitable
7. irritable
8. charitable
9. memorable
10. comparable
11. probable
12. reasonable

Week 15 Day 1 (page 96)

1. infallible
2. feasible
3. indestructible
4. convertible
5. incredible
6. indelible
7. irreversible
8. compatible
9. distractible
10. invisible
11. irresistible
12. illegible

Week 15 Day 2 (page 97)

1. invisible
2. incredible
3. infallible
4. eligible
5. illegible
6. indelible
7. distractible
8. indestructible
9. feasible
10. compatible
11. irresistible
12. convertible

Week 15 Day 3 (page 98)

1. flex
2. flexible
3. flexibility
4. inflexible
5. deflect
6. reflect
7. reflection
8. reflector
9. reflex
10. inflection
11. reflective

Week 15 Day 4 (page 99)

Responses must include bolded words.

Week 15 Day 5 (page 100)

1. illegible
2. impossible
3. indelible
4. convertible
5. invincible
6. inflexible
7. distractible
8. responsible
9. reversible
10. compatible
11. incredible
12. invisible

Answer Key (cont.)

Week 16 Day 1 (page 102)

1.	exotic	7.	authentic
2.	democratic	8.	academic
3.	economics	9.	automatic
4.	sympathetic	10.	epidemic
5.	Arctic	11.	antibiotic
6.	aerobic	12.	domestic

Week 16 Day 2 (page 103)

1.	traumatic	7.	domestic
2.	pathetic	8.	dramatic
3.	exotic	9.	antibiotic
4.	automatic	10.	Arctic
5.	authentic	11.	majestic
6.	energetic	12.	epidemic

Week 16 Day 3 (page 104)

1.	empathize	7.	apathy
2.	empathy	8.	pathetic
3.	empathetic	9.	passion
4.	sympathize	10.	passionate
5.	sympathy	11.	compassion
6.	sympathetic	12.	compassionate

Week 16 Day 4 (page 105)

Responses must include bolded words.

Week 16 Day 5 (page 106)

1.	Antarctic	7.	energetic
2.	democratic	8.	domestic
3.	aerobic	9.	antibiotic
4.	epidemic	10.	Arctic
5.	academic	11.	patriotic
6.	ceramic	12.	exotic

Week 17 Day 1 (page 108)

1.	terminal	7.	interval
2.	maternal	8.	numeral
3.	rehearsal	9.	intentional
4.	perpetual	10.	hysterical
5.	critical	11.	alphabetical
6.	collateral	12.	emotional

Week 17 Day 2 (page 109)

1.	hysterical	7.	horizontal
2.	perpetual	8.	emotional
3.	universal	9.	carnival
4.	critical	10.	interval
5.	intentional	11.	practical
6.	literal	12.	rehearsal

Week 17 Day 3 (page 110)

1.	maternal	7.	paternity
2.	maternity	8.	patriarch
3.	matriarch	9.	patron
4.	matron	10.	patriot
5.	matrimony	11.	patriotic
6.	paternal		

Week 17 Day 4 (page 111)

Responses must include bolded words.

Week 17 Day 5 (page 112)

1.	paternal	7.	international
2.	nocturnal	8.	horizontal
3.	carnival	9.	intentional
4.	rehearsal	10.	universal
5.	literal	11.	numeral
6.	hysterical	12.	perpetual

Week 18 Day 1 (page 114)

1.	significant	7.	occupancy
2.	discrepancy	8.	abundant
3.	resistant	9.	arrogance
4.	vacancy	10.	insurance
5.	reluctant	11.	defiant
6.	maintenance	12.	redundant

Week 18 Day 2 (page 115)

1.	endurance	7.	arrogance
2.	maintenance	8.	reluctant
3.	abundant	9.	extravagant
4.	buoyancy	10.	discrepancy
5.	ignorant	11.	insurance
6.	defiant	12.	redundant

Week 18 Day 3 (page 116)

1.	sign	7.	designer
2.	signature	8.	assign
3.	signal	9.	assignment
4.	significant	10.	resign
5.	insignificant	11.	consign
6.	significance	12.	designate

Week 18 Day 4 (page 117)

1. *Ignorance is bliss:* It's better to not know what's going on, so you can be less stressed and worried.
2. *Within striking distance:* close to a desired goal or objective
3. *The elephant in the room:* an awkward but obvious topic that no one wants to talk about.
4. *A picture is worth a thousand words:* It's much easier to express an idea with a picture than it is to describe it with words.

Week 18 Day 5 (page 118)

1.	pregnancy	7.	observant
2.	defiant	8.	ignorant
3.	attendance	9.	abundant
4.	appliance	10.	endurance
5.	vacancy	11.	arrogance
6.	extravagant	12.	insurance

Week 19 Day 1 (page 120)

1.	interference	7.	eloquent
2.	indifferent	8.	persistent
3.	incompetent	9.	equivalent
4.	apparent	10.	turbulence
5.	presidency	11.	superintendent
6.	affluent	12.	frequency

Week 19 Day 2 (page 121)

1.	independence	7.	permanent
2.	affluent	8.	equivalent
3.	competent	9.	eloquent
4.	apparent	10.	persistent
5.	condolences	11.	indifferent
6.	prevalent	12.	consequence

Answer Key (cont.)

Week 19 Day 3 (page 122)

1. resist
2. resistance
3. irresistible
4. assist
5. assistant
6. assistance
7. consists
8. consistent
9. inconsistent
10. persist
11. persistent
12. insist

Week 19 Day 4 (page 123)

1. *Absence makes the heart grow fonder:* When the people we love are far away, we love and miss them even more.
2. *Innocent until proven guilty:* A person cannot be punished until a jury proves the person committed a crime.
3. *Silence is golden:* It is sometimes smarter to say nothing.
4. *Different strokes for different folks:* People like different things and live in different ways.

Week 19 Day 5 (page 124)

1. condolences
2. frequency
3. consistency
4. superintendent
5. turbulence
6. permanent
7. equivalent
8. independence
9. interference
10. consequence
11. indifferent
12. presidency

Week 20 Day 1 (page 126)

1. inanimate
2. unfortunate
3. immaculate
4. legitimate
5. moderate
6. approximate
7. coordinate
8. desolate
9. advocate
10. inappropriate
11. illiterate
12. intricate

Week 20 Day 2 (page 127)

1. affectionate
2. adequate
3. immaculate
4. articulate
5. unfortunate
6. inanimate
7. intricate
8. legitimate
9. advocate
10. moderate
11. desolate
12. associate

Week 20 Day 3 (page 128)

1. reply
2. complicate
3. complicated
4. apply
5. application
6. duplicate
7. replicate
8. multiply
9. imply
10. pliable
11. explicit
12. implicit

Week 20 Day 4 (page 129)

Answers should be a paragraph and use a minimum of six –*ate* words.

Week 20 Day 5 (page 130)

1. vertebrate
2. inanimate
3. immaculate
4. associate
5. duplicate
6. illiterate
7. intermediate
8. unfortunate
9. intricate
10. coordinates
11. desolate
12. moderate

Week 21 Day 1 (page 132)

1. humidity
2. security
3. electricity
4. opportunity
5. authority
6. intensity
7. facility
8. fidelity
9. capacity
10. necessity
11. priority
12. responsibility

Week 21 Day 2 (page 133)

1. security
2. intensity
3. authority
4. nationality
5. necessity
6. hostility
7. curiosity
8. fidelity
9. humidity
10. university
11. facility
12. opportunity

Week 21 Day 3 (page 134)

1. confide
2. fidelity
3. confident
4. confidence
5. confidant
6. confidential
7. diffident
8. diffidence
9. affidavit
10. Fido
11. infidel
12. bona fide

Week 21 Day 4 (page 135)

1. *Variety is the spice of life:* Having lots of different experiences is what makes life interesting and enjoyable.
2. *In the middle of difficulty lies opportunity:* People often learn and accomplish the most when they're struggling with a difficult problem or situation.
3. *Curiosity killed the cat:* Being too nosy about other people's business will get you in trouble.
4. *Necessity is the mother of invention:* When we have a problem that needs to be solved, we find creative ways to solve it.

Week 21 Day 5 (page 136)

1. equality
2. nationality
3. humidity
4. university
5. capacity
6. electricity
7. personality
8. necessity
9. hostility
10. responsibility
11. intensity
12. possibility

Week 22 Day 1 (page 138)

1. commentary
2. monetary
3. hereditary
4. obituary
5. sanitary
6. extraordinary
7. documentary
8. itinerary
9. complimentary
10. customary
11. revolutionary
12. salivary

Week 22 Day 2 (page 139)

1. hereditary
2. monetary
3. culinary
4. vocabulary
5. imaginary
6. involuntary
7. exemplary
8. customary
9. sanitary
10. itinerary
11. complimentary
12. capillary

Week 22 Day 3 (page 140)

1. malevolent
2. benevolent
3. volunteer
4. voluntary
5. involuntary
6. infirmary
7. confirm
8. confirmation
9. unconfirmed
10. affirm
11. reaffirm
12. affirmation

Week 22 Day 4 (page 141)

Responses must include bolded words.

Answer Key *(cont.)*

Week 22 Day 5 (page 142)

1. imaginary
2. infirmary
3. capillary
4. obituary
5. hereditary
6. revolutionary
7. itinerary
8. anniversary
9. extraordinary
10. complimentary
11. vocabulary
12. culinary

Week 23 Day 1 (page 144)

1. laboratory
2. circulatory
3. trajectory
4. self-explanatory
5. lavatory
6. discriminatory
7. contradictory
8. inflammatory
9. accessory
10. accusatory
11. obligatory
12. observatory

Week 23 Day 2 (page 145)

1. obligatory
2. trajectory
3. lavatory
4. inflammatory
5. derogatory
6. self-explanatory
7. discriminatory
8. satisfactory
9. dormitory
10. predatory
11. accessories
12. introductory

Week 23 Day 3 (page 146)

1. injection
2. eject
3. rejection
4. interject
5. projector
6. project
7. object
8. objection
9. trajectory
10. subject
11. projectile
12. conjecture

Week 23 Day 5 (page 148)

1. laboratory
2. lavatory
3. respiratory
4. dormitory
5. auditory
6. introductory
7. satisfactory
8. derogatory
9. accessory
10. accusatory
11. migratory
12. self-explanatory

Week 24 Day 1 (page 150)

1. frivolous
2. indigenous
3. ominous
4. miraculous
5. meticulous
6. ludicrous
7. omnivorous
8. prosperous
9. autonomous
10. unanimous
11. adventurous
12. perilous

Week 24 Day 2 (page 151)

1. indigenous
2. ominous
3. unanimous
4. ludicrous
5. prosperous
6. villainous
7. perilous
8. frivolous
9. meticulous
10. mountainous
11. autonomous
12. miraculous

Week 24 Day 3 (page 152)

1. autobiography
2. autobiographical
3. automobile
4. automotive
5. automatic
6. autograph
7. autonomy
8. autonomous
9. autopilot
10. autoimmune
11. autopsy
12. automated

Week 24 Day 4 (page 153)

Responses must include bolded words.

Week 24 Day 5 (page 154)

1. carnivorous
2. mountainous
3. unanimous
4. ridiculous
5. adventurous
6. villainous
7. frivolous
8. disastrous
9. indigenous
10. herbivorous
11. synonymous
12. mischievous

Week 25 Day 1 (page 156)

1. mythology
2. apology
3. technology
4. intriguing
5. disadvantage
6. geologist
7. psychologist
8. epilogue
9. monologue
10. terminology
11. ecology
12. archaeology

Week 25 Day 2 (page 157)

1. zoology
2. meteorology
3. geologist
4. apology
5. intriguing
6. disadvantage
7. epilogue
8. chronology
9. mythology
10. terminology
11. synagogue
12. technology

Week 25 Day 3 (page 158)

1. zoology
2. geology
3. psychology
4. ecology
5. meteorology
6. biology
7. archaeology
8. technology
9. chronology
10. mythology
11. analogy
12. apology

Week 25 Day 4 (page 159)

Responses must include bolded words.

Week 25 Day 5 (page 160)

1. synagogue
2. apology
3. biology
4. mythology
5. epilogue
6. monologue
7. psychologist
8. meteorology
9. intriguing
10. technology
11. disadvantage
12. archaeology

Week 26 Day 1 (page 162)

1. experiment
2. ulterior
3. severity
4. inferior
5. posterior
6. deteriorate
7. interior
8. serial
9. criteria
10. bacteria
11. clerical
12. material

Week 26 Day 2 (page 163)

1. severity
2. material
3. deteriorate
4. mysterious
5. superior
6. experience
7. exterior
8. posterior
9. period
10. cafeteria
11. bacteria
12. ulterior

Week 26 Day 3 (page 164)

1. exterior
2. interior
3. anterior
4. posterior
5. ulterior
6. superior
7. superiority
8. inferior
9. inferiority
10. senior
11. seniority
12. deteriorate

Answer Key (cont.)

Week 26 Day 5 (page 166)

1. period
2. material
3. experiment
4. superior
5. imperial
6. exterior
7. cafeteria
8. bacteria
9. clerical
10. interior
11. anterior
12. criteria

Week 27 Day 1 (page 168)

1. humiliate
2. marsupial
3. portfolio
4. radiant
5. alleviate
6. recipient
7. menial
8. equilibrium
9. memorial
10. idiosyncrasies
11. colonial
12. idiom

Week 27 Day 2 (page 169)

1. radiant
2. humiliate
3. alleviate
4. idiom
5. audience
6. equilibrium
7. trivial
8. menial
9. custodian
10. radius
11. memorial
12. recipient

Week 27 Day 3 (page 170)

1. radiate
2. radiation
3. radio
4. radiant
5. radius
6. radiology
7. equilibrium
8. equitable
9. adequate
10. inadequate
11. equator
12. equation

Week 27 Day 4 (page 171)

Responses must include bolded words.

Week 27 Day 5 (page 172)

1. idiom
2. custodian
3. audience
4. portfolio
5. recipient
6. trivial
7. podium
8. radius
9. marsupial
10. nutrients
11. gymnasium
12. alleviate

Week 28 Day 1 (page 174)

1. specialty
2. association
3. judicious
4. unconscious
5. beneficial
6. malicious
7. suspicious
8. depreciate
9. atrocious
10. insufficient
11. pediatrician
12. sociable

Week 28 Day 2 (page 175)

1. judicious
2. atrocious
3. depreciate
4. beneficial
5. appreciation
6. malicious
7. sociable
8. insufficient
9. association
10. pediatrician
11. suspicious
12. electrician

Week 28 Day 3 (page 176)

1. politician
2. mathematician
3. pediatrician
4. electrician
5. statistician
6. technician
7. magician
8. musician
9. physician
10. optician
11. pediatrician
12. magician
13. mathematician
14. politician
15. electrician
16. physician
17. technician
18. musician

Week 28 Day 4 (page 177)

Responses must include bolded words.

Week 28 Day 5 (page 178)

1. pediatrician
2. magician
3. electrician
4. appreciation
5. musician
6. unconscious
7. politician
8. physician
9. mathematician
10. beneficial
11. malicious
12. depreciate

Week 29 Day 1 (page 180)

1. gorgeous
2. ambitious
3. outrageous
4. anxious
5. miscellaneous
6. rambunctious
7. prestigious
8. spontaneous
9. superstitious
10. victorious
11. religious
12. igneous

Week 29 Day 2 (page 181)

1. courageous
2. miscellaneous
3. hilarious
4. rambunctious
5. spontaneous
6. cautious
7. anxious
8. nutritious
9. prestigious
10. scrumptious
11. contagious
12. igneous

Week 29 Day 3 (page 182)

1. tangible
2. intangible
3. contiguous
4. contagious
5. contact
6. intact
7. tactful
8. tact
9. tactile
10. tangent
11. tango
12. contingent

Week 29 Day 4 (page 183)

Answers should include six comments and use a minimum of six –ous words.

Week 29 Day 5 (page 184)

1. nutritious
2. courageous
3. cautious
4. religious
5. igneous
6. anxious
7. victorious
8. ambitious
9. contagious
10. scrumptious
11. hilarious
12. prestigious

Week 30 Day 1 (page 186)

1. preferential
2. negotiate
3. sequential
4. influential
5. residential
6. partial
7. essential
8. substantial
9. controversial
10. credential
11. initiative
12. potential

Week 30 Day 2 (page 187)

1. essential
2. confidential
3. controversial
4. negotiate
5. sequential
6. patience
7. partial
8. substantial
9. Christian
10. Asian
11. residential
12. credential

Answer Key (cont.)

Week 30 Day 3 (page 188)

1. fluent	7. influence
2. fluency	8. influential
3. affluent	9. flush
4. affluence	10. flux
5. fluid	11. influx
6. fluctuate	12. reflux

Week 30 Day 4 (page 189)

Responses must include bolded words.

Week 30 Day 5 (page 190)

1. patient	7. sequential
2. residential	8. controversial
3. initial	9. Christian
4. Asian	10. negotiate
5. quotient	11. essential
6. torrential	12. confidential

Week 31 Day 1 (page 192)

1. clique	7. unique
2. opaque	8. banquet
3. delinquent	9. oblique
4. etiquette	10. technique
5. mosque	11. picturesque
6. plaque	12. boutique

Week 31 Day 2 (page 193)

1. technique	7. unique
2. etiquette	8. acquaintance
3. delinquent	9. plaque
4. conquer	10. mosque
5. antique	11. oblique
6. opaque	12. picturesque

Week 31 Day 3 (page 194)

1. critic	7. hypocrite
2. critical	8. crisis
3. criticize	9. technique
4. criticism	10. technical
5. criteria	11. technology
6. critique	12. technician

Week 31 Day 4 (page 195)

Responses must include bolded words.

Week 31 Day 5 (page 196)

1. clique	7. plaque
2. tourniquet	8. grotesque
3. mosque	9. croquet
4. boutique	10. antique
5. opaque	11. oblique
6. bouquet	12. conquer

Week 32 Day 1 (page 198)

1. allegiance	7. strategy
2. prodigious	8. generic
3. indulgent	9. pungent
4. negligent	10. agility
5. allergen	11. nostalgic
6. congenital	12. digital

Week 32 Day 2 (page 199)

1. diligent	7. prodigious
2. negligent	8. pungent
3. congenital	9. generosity
4. allegiance	10. nostalgic
5. generic	11. detergent
6. indulgent	12. strategy

Week 32 Day 3 (page 200)

1. legal	7. delegate
2. illegal	8. diligent
3. legislature	9. negligent
4. legislator	10. elegant
5. legitimate	11. eligible
6. privilege	12. intelligent

Week 32 Day 5 (page 202)

1. detergent	7. nostalgic
2. geometry	8. digital
3. allergen	9. legislature
4. regional	10. manageable
5. agility	11. indulgent
6. pungent	12. legendary

Week 33 Day 1 (page 204)

1. triumphant	7. esophagus
2. phenomenon	8. catastrophe
3. metamorphosis	9. decipher
4. apostrophe	10. sophisticated
5. peripheral	11. philosophy
6. sophomore	12. photosynthesis

Week 33 Day 2 (page 205)

1. catastrophe	7. pharmacist
2. peripheral	8. amphibian
3. triumphant	9. apostrophe
4. phenomenon	10. esophagus
5. decipher	11. sophomore
6. sophisticated	12. metamorphosis

Week 33 Day 3 (page 206)

1. photograph	7. sophomore
2. photography	8. philosophy
3. photographer	9. philosopher
4. photogenic	10. philosophical
5. photocopy	11. sophisticated
6. photosynthesis	12. unsophisticated

Week 33 Day 4 (page 207)

Responses must include bolded words.

Week 33 Day 5 (page 208)

1. sophomore	7. physical
2. amphibian	8. xylophone
3. geography	9. photographer
4. apostrophe	10. catastrophe
5. biography	11. decipher
6. photocopy	12. pharmacist

Week 34 Day 1 (page 210)

1. descendant	7. accessible
2. susceptible	8. coincidence
3. reminisce	9. convalescent
4. publicity	10. circumstances
5. condescending	11. fascination
6. eccentric	12. accentuate

Week 34 Day 2 (page 211)

1. reminisce	7. accidentally
2. adolescent	8. susceptible
3. accessible	9. eccentric
4. necessary	10. succinctly
5. accentuate	11. publicity
6. descendant	12. celebrity

Answer Key (cont.)

Week 34 Day 3 (page 212)

1. convalescent
2. adolescent
3. fluorescent
4. ascend
5. descend
6. descendant
7. condescending
8. accident
9. accidentally
10. incident
11. coincidence
12. coincidentally

Week 34 Day 4 (page 213)

1. *Practice what you preach:* Don't be a hypocrite. Make sure your words and actions go together.
2. *Honesty is the best policy:* It's always better to tell the truth.
3. *Laughter is the best medicine:* Our minds and bodies feel better when we laugh and try to focus on positive things.
4. *Success has many fathers, while failure is an orphan:* Everyone wants to take credit for good ideas, but no one wants to take the blame when things go wrong.

Week 34 Day 5 (page 214)

1. adolescent
2. descendant
3. fluorescent
4. reminisce
5. celebration
6. convalescent
7. accentuate
8. susceptible
9. scientific
10. circumstance
11. necessary
12. coincidence

Week 35 Day 1 (page 216)

1. characteristics
2. choreograph
3. chronic
4. technical
5. chaos
6. monarch
7. charisma
8. archives
9. chronological
10. architect
11. scholarship
12. chemical

Week 35 Day 2 (page 217)

1. chaos
2. arachnid
3. characteristics
4. technical
5. chronological
6. charisma
7. chronic
8. bronchitis
9. character
10. scholarship
11. chameleon
12. choreograph

Week 35 Day 3 (page 218)

1. synchronize
2. chronology
3. chronological
4. chronic
5. chronicle
6. monarch
7. matriarch
8. patriarch
9. architect
10. anarchy
11. hierarchy
12. archive

Week 35 Day 4 (page 219)

Responses must include bolded words.

Week 35 Day 5 (page 220)

1. chemistry
2. arachnid
3. architect
4. scholarship
5. mechanic
6. chrysalis
7. choreograph
8. orchestra
9. chronological
10. character
11. archive
12. monarch

Week 36 Day 1 (page 222)

1. chaperone
2. chivalrous
3. nonchalant
4. cliché
5. chiffon
6. brochure
7. chalet
8. chagrin
9. fuchsia
10. quiche
11. chandelier
12. charade

Week 36 Day 2 (page 223)

1. chagrin
2. chauffeur
3. cliché
4. brochure
5. chivalrous
6. chef
7. nonchalant
8. Michigan
9. chalet
10. chandelier
11. chiffon
12. pistachio

Week 36 Day 3 (page 224)

1. dermatology
2. dermatologist
3. epidermis
4. pachyderm
5. cardiology
6. cardiologist
7. cardiac
8. corporation
9. corporate
10. incorporate

Week 36 Day 4 (page 225)

Responses must include bolded words.

Week 36 Day 5 (page 226)

1. fuchsia
2. Chicago
3. Michigan
4. chaperone
5. chauffeur
6. mustache
7. chandelier
8. brochure
9. chef
10. cliché
11. pistachio
12. crochet

Unit Assessments

At the end of each unit, use the corresponding quiz to determine what students have learned. Ask students to spell the two words. Then, have students write the sentence. Say the words and sentence slowly, repeating as often as needed. The bolded words were studied in the unit.

Unit	Phonetic Pattern	Words	Sentence
1	short *a* words	abdicate, aptitude	We expressed **gratitude** to the **astronauts** for their many **sacrifices**.
2	short *e* words	escalate, televise	They **excavated** the work site, **investigated** soil samples, and looked for **specimens**.
3	short *i* words	relinquish, restrictions	Why did members of the **committee criticize** the old **curriculum**?
4	more short *i* words	mystery, sycamore	Is it **typical** for **gymnastics** gear to be made from **synthetic** fabric?
5	short *o* words	confiscate, modernize	It's hard to **comprehend** how many **obstacles** people face when they struggle with **poverty**.
6	*ar* pattern	department, parasol	Due to the **aquarium's popularity**, visitors had to wait in a long line near the penguin **area**.
7	*r*-controlled vowels	portfolio, reversal	Why do customers **purposely** knock over the **merchandise** after I **organize** it on the shelf?
8	*–ment* ending	endorsement, retirement	There was a lot of **excitement** when people saw the **advertisement** for the new shopping **development**.
9	*–ive* ending	cohesive, progressively	Some children get too **aggressive** and use **excessive** force when they play **competitive** sports.
10	*–ar, –er,* and *–or* endings	abductor, vascular	My boss is very **particular**, so she hired an **engineer** to design a new kind of **elevator** for our building.
11	*–ation* ending	exclamation, respiration	The **invitation** includes **information** about different **transportation** options.
12	more *–tion* endings	evolution, ratification	Fill out the **application**, and we'll see if you have the right **qualifications** to join our **institution**.
13	*–sion* ending	indecision, recession	Why were you full of **apprehension** when you watched the funeral **procession** on **television**?
14	*–able* ending	expendable, irreplaceable	The cost is **reasonable**, and the practices are **manageable**, but the distance we're expected to travel for games is **unbelievable**!
15	*–ible* ending	admissible, incompatible	Mom bought me a **reversible** comforter that is **indestructible** and **irresistible**.
16	*–ic* ending	apathetic, fantastic	The **antibiotic** had a **dramatic** effect on Kate's symptoms and helped her feel more **energetic**.
17	*–al* ending	functional, mythical	Some people were **emotional** when they said goodbye to their families at the **international terminal**.
18	*–ant* and *–ance* endings	dominant, significance	There was a **vacancy** at the **extravagant** hotel, and the amenities were **abundant**.
19	*–ent* and *–ence* endings	decency, inconsistent	**Apparently, turbulence** is so **prevalen**t it doesn't even bother flight attendants.

Unit	Phonetic Pattern	Words	Sentence
20	*–ate* ending	conglomerate, subordinates	It's **unfortunate** that there is not an **adequate** supply of water in the **desolate** region of the state.
21	*–ity* ending	nobility, simplicity	If I get the **opportunity** to attend a **university**, studying will be my **priority**.
22	*–ary* ending	contemporary, missionary	The **itinerary** for my parents' **anniversary** trip includes three **culinary** classes.
23	*–ory* ending	conservatory, repertory	Why did you make **derogatory** and **inflammatory** remarks about the men who work in the **laboratory**?
24	*–ous* ending	scrupulous, torturous	A pair of **adventurous** hikers took a **perilous** trip through the **mountainous** region.
25	hard and soft *g* words	anthology, catalogue	**Geologists** have uncovered **intriguing** facts about the past thanks to modern **technology**.
26	*eri* pattern	sincerity, hysteria	Why are the **interior** walls of the **cafeteria** starting to **deteriorate**?
27	more *i* patterns that sound like *e*	comedian, convivial	Please ask the **custodian** to set up the **podium** in the **gymnasium**.
28	*ci* words	optician, precocious	A **pediatrician** is a **physician** whose **specialty** is caring for children.
29	*–eous* and *–ious* endings	infectious, simultaneous	Mom packed **nutritious** snacks and **miscellaneous** toys to keep my brother happy during our drive through the **gorgeous** countryside.
30	more *ti* and *si* patterns	presidential, Russian	We tried to **negotiate** a refund after a **substantial** portion of our campsite was flooded by the **torrential** rain.
31	*qu* pattern	acquitted, bisque	Is it considered proper **etiquette** to bring the coach a **bouquet** of flowers at the **banquet**?
32	more soft *g* words	margarine, passengers	Looking at Nate's **prodigious** collection of baseball cards makes me **nostalgic** about my **legendary** season on the minor league team.
33	*ph* words	atmosphere, photogenic	If **pharmacists** don't **decipher** prescriptions correctly, they can cause a life or death **catastrophe**.
34	more soft *c* patterns	effervescent, vaccinated	It's **necessary** to wash your hands before you visit a **convalescent** home because the residents are very **susceptible** to illness.
35	hard *ch* words	anachronism, matriarch	Zach earned a **scholarship** to study **mechanics** at a **technical** school.
36	soft *ch* words	chevron, chaparral	The bride and groom ate **pistachios** while the **chauffeur** drove them around **Chicago**.

Spelling Categories

Spelling Category	Spelling Pattern	Unit
Short Vowels	short *a* words	1
	short *e* words	2
	short *i* words	3
	more short *i* words	4
	short o words	5
R-Controlled Vowels	*ar* pattern	6
	r-controlled vowels	7
	eri pattern	26
Hard and Soft Consonants	hard and soft *g* words	25
	ci words	28
	more *ti* and *si* patterns	30
	qu pattern	31
	more soft *g* words	32
	more soft c patterns	34
Consonant Digraphs	*ph* words	33
	hard *ch* words	35
	soft *ch* words	36
Ambiguous Vowels	more *i* patterns that sound like *e*	27
Final Syllables	–*ment* ending	8
	–*ive* ending	9
	–*ar*, –*er*, and –*or* endings	10
	–*ation* ending	11
	more –*tion* endings	12
	–*sion* ending	13
	–*able* ending	14
	–*ible* ending	15
	–*ic* ending	16
	–*al* ending	17
	–*ant* and –*ance* endings	18
	–*ent* and –*ence* endings	19
	–*ate* ending	20
	–*ity* ending	21
	–*ary* ending	22
	–*ory* ending	23
	–*ous* ending	24
	–*eous* and –*ious* endings	29

© *Shell Education*   *28634—180 Days of Spelling and Word Study*   239

Digital Resources

Accessing the Digital Resources

The digital resources can be downloaded by following these steps:

1. Go to **www.tcmpub.com/digital**

2. Sign in or create an account.

3. Click **Redeem Content** and enter the ISBN number, located on page 2 and the back cover, into the appropriate field on the website.

4. Respond to the prompts using the book to view your account and available digital content.

5. Choose the digital resources you would like to download. You can download all the files at once, or you can download a specific group of files.

ISBN:
9781425833145

Please note: Some files provided for download have large file sizes. Download times for these larger files will vary based on your download speed.

 ## Contents of the Digital Resources

Teaching Resources Folder

- Additional Spelling Activities

- Additional Word Lists (below and on grade level)

- Unit Overview Pages

Assessments Folder

- Analysis Charts separated by spelling category

- Unit Assessments (pages 237–238)

- Assessment Reproducible
